# Pop-Up
## paper structures

The Beginner's Guide to Creating
3-D Elements for Books, Cards & More

## Heidi Pridemore

C&T PUBLISHING

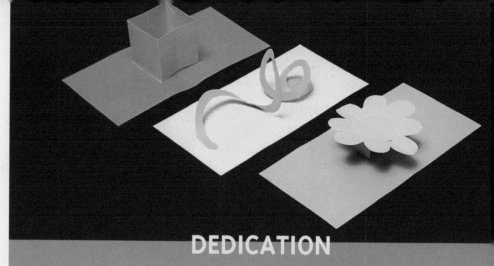

Text © 2007 Heidi Pridemore

Artwork © 2007 C&T Publishing, Inc.

Publisher: Amy Marson

Editorial Director: Gailen Runge

Acquisitions Editor: Jan Grigsby

Editor: Stacy Chamness

Copyeditor/Proofreader: Wordfirm Inc.

Cover Designer/Book Designer: Christina D. Jarumay

Production Coordinator: Kirstie L. Pettersen

Illustrator: Tim Manibusan

Photography by C&T Publishing, Inc., unless otherwise noted

Published by C&T Publishing, Inc., P.O. Box 1456, Lafayette, CA 94549

**Library of Congress Cataloging-in-Publication Data**

Pridemore, Heidi.

Pop-up paper structures : the beginner's guide to creating 3-D elements for books, cards & more / Heidi Pridemore.

p. cm.

ISBN-13: 978-1-57120-420-2 (paper trade : alk. paper)

ISBN-10: 1-57120-420-2 (paper trade : alk. paper)

1. Paper work. 2. Three-dimensional greeting cards. 3. Toy and movable books. I. Title.

TT870.P762 2007

745.54'2—dc22

2006034228

10 9 8 7 6 5 4 3 2 1

# DEDICATION

I would like to dedicate this book to Mary Kortemeyer, my mentor and dear friend. Mary hired me fresh out of college as an eager, untrained designer. She took a chance on me as an employee, and in turn we each gained a lifelong friend.

Mary taught me how to be a professional designer and introduced me to many of the skills I would later use to start my own business. But more important, she taught me that I could do anything I put my mind to and that no dream is ever out of reach if I work hard enough.

I will continue to chase after—and hopefully catch—more of my dreams in honor of her memory.

# ACKNOWLEDGMENTS

I would like to thank everyone who has helped make this book possible:

- My family and friends continually supported me personally and professionally. I would not be here without each one of them.

- Jan Grigsby at C&T Publishing offered me this project, and Stacy, Luke, Christina, Kirstie, and Tim helped make this book the best it can be.

- Emily Cohen remembered my experiences with paper engineering and recommended me to C&T Publishing.

- Susan and Freddie Weltman supported me when I was starting out and over the years. They have become wonderful friends to my family and me. I also thank their company, American Pin/HyGlo, for donating so many of the products I used for the projects in this book.

- Sharon Cheng and Stacey Ann Lorish helped with creating samples for the book.

- A special thank you goes to my husband, Matthew, who keeps me sane when things get crazy. He encourages me to reach for the stars and supports me every step of the way.

# INTRODUCTION

op-up artwork entertains and delights children and adults alike. These movable pieces of art are visually stunning, and they intrigue the viewer, causing many to wonder how they work. What makes them pop up? This question is exactly what gets many "paper engineers" started in making pop-ups. Each pop-up is a mystery just waiting to be solved. Anyone with patience and a willingness to learn can create these little paper mysteries!

This book was designed to be a starting point for a beginner interested in learning the basics of creating pop-ups, and I have put the techniques in order of ease. I'll cover the basic pop-up techniques, and you can build on these to create more-advanced pop-ups!

All the pop-ups are based on a set of rules that need to be followed for the pop-up to work. Once you have a good understanding of these rules, expanding on these techniques to create your own pop-ups is easy. I have included the technical information and basic pop-up rules to help budding paper engineers move beyond this book and create their own pop-ups.

Start at the beginning of the book and read the information on the papers and tools. When you are ready to begin your first project, be sure to read the Creating Pop-Ups chapter (page 10) first. This chapter defines pop-up terms and provides helpful how-to instructions and tips that apply to the majority of the pop-ups.

# table of

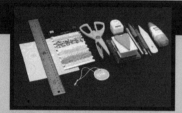

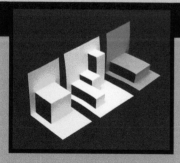

# contents

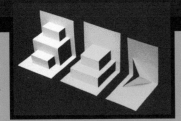

# CHAPTER 1

# The Basics

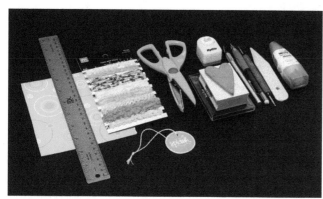

You need only a few tools to begin making pop-up art, but there are many other tools and products available that you can use to enhance your pieces!

## THE PAPER

Without paper there would be no pop-ups! Choosing the paper for each project is the most important step. Many types of papers are available today, and each type of paper reacts differently to being creased, folded, and glued.

As a beginner, you'll need to understand the differences between the types of paper available and which type will work best for a particular project. When I started making pop-ups, there were few paper types to choose

from—standard office paper, white cardstock, or expensive handmade and art papers available through art stores. Because of the growth of the paper craft and scrapbooking markets in the past few years, there is now an entire rainbow of colors and prints on assorted types of paper to choose from.

When looking for a good pop-up art paper, you need to consider a couple things:

■ **The paper has to hold a fold.**

Thick papers do not hold a fold well. Watercolor paper is a good example; its texture is closer to that of fabric.

■ **The paper has to have some elasticity.**

The paper has to open and stretch to hold the pop-up shape and then close flat again to its original form. Some papers, such as vellum, hold a fold but do not stretch.

Here is a general overview of some types of paper that are available, with comments on how each type works for pop-ups. When trying a paper that is not listed here, start with a small practice piece to see how the paper handles. Test how easy it is to mark, cut, fold, manipulate, and glue before investing a lot of time on the final project.

**Cardstock** Medium-weight cardstock is my favorite to work with. Several types of cardstock are available in just about any color imaginable, many of which are acid free. Cardstock cuts and folds nicely and glues together quickly. Cardstock isn't as thin as copy paper, and its thickness makes cardstock more durable.

**High-Gloss Cardstock** Most high-gloss cardstock has a white core, which can show when the cardstock is scored and folded. In some cases, the white color can become a design feature of the piece, but you may not want this effect in your pop-up.

Cardstock with color throughout and high-gloss cardstock with a white core

**Textured Cardstock** Many of the textured cardstocks work for pop-ups. The exception is cardstock with deeply embossed lines. These embossed lines act like the lines you will score on your pop-ups, so the paper will want to fold on the embossed lines. This type of card-stock can be tricky to fold, but patience and experience will keep you from getting frustrated.

**Copy Paper** Copy paper is good for practice. Standard copy paper comes in several varieties and colors. It is easy to cut and fold, and it glues together nicely. Unfortunately, this paper is not acid free and will yellow and age over time. So copy paper is perfect for practice but not the best choice for your masterpiece.

**Printed Acid-Free Paper** Printed acid-free paper usually comes in 12″ squares and is found in the scrapbooking department of stores. These sheets are generally printed on only one side, although more companies are producing double-sided papers.

**tip**

*Remember that in most pop-up pieces, both sides of the paper show. Be sure that you are happy with the color on both sides of whichever paper you use.*

**Printed Vellum** Printed vellum works with certain pop-ups. Vellum doesn't have much elasticity and doesn't always hold the shape of the pop-up. Vellum works best in the 90° single-sheet techniques. Test different pop-up techniques to see how vellum performs.

**Embossed Vellum** Embossed vellum has the same pitfalls of embossed cardstock, along with the problems of working with vellum.

**Acetate** Acetate is a thin film. The main drawback of working with films is that draft marks tend to show in the final piece. Also, you need to use an adhesive that dries clear, or it will show through the film. These are the only difficulties of working with acetate, printed or not.

# THE TOOLS

**Craft Knife and Extra Blades** To create pop-up pieces, you have to cut slots in the center of a page or cut around shapes without damaging the background paper. A size #11 craft knife has a sharp tip and makes cutting precisely on drawn lines easy. A craft knife with a sharp blade works best. A dull blade can tear the paper or, more dangerously, jump across the paper and cut the user. Depending on the material you are working with, a blade will last for maybe two small projects or one large project. (For example, a blade will become dull faster when cutting cardstock or cardboard than when cutting paper.)

**Self-Healing Cutting Mat** A self-healing cutting mat heals after you cut on it with a craft knife. Many brands in a variety of sizes are available. Before you purchase one, think about the size of the projects you will be making. I find that a 12″ × 18″ mat made for use with a craft knife is large enough for most papercraft projects. Many of the cutting mats designed for quilters to use with rotary cutters are not thick enough for prolonged use with a craft knife.

**tip**

*Making pop-ups with kids? An adult should make any craft blade cuts; then let the kids assemble and decorate the pop-ups!*

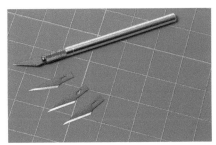

Size #11 craft knife, extra blades, and a self-healing cutting mat

### Metal Ruler With Cork Backing

Lines must be cut straight and to the desired measurements. Precision is very important in paper engineering. A craft knife works best with a metal ruler, and the cork backing keeps the ruler from sliding across the surface of the paper. The size you'll need depends on the projects you'll be working on. I like a 12″ ruler for most projects.

### T-Square

A T-square is made up of two straight edges oriented perpendicular to each other, forming a T. T-squares allow you to draw or cut a line perpendicular to another line or edge. Metal T-squares with a ruler printed on the straight edge are available, thus eliminating the need for a separate metal ruler.

**tip**

*Like all types of engineering, paper engineering requires the right tools for precision!*

Metal ruler and T-square

### Creasing Tools

A *ball stylus tool,* a *bone folder,* or a sewer's *point turner and seam creaser* will make crease lines on paper. I prefer the ball stylus tool, but that is purely a personal preference. I recommend trying all and deciding which one works best for you.

**tip**

*Don't have a creasing tool handy? Try using an empty ballpoint pen.*

A bone folder, a point turner and creasing tool, and a ball stylus tool

### Mechanical Pencil

All pop-ups need to be sketched before they are cut and assembled. The draft lines need to be thin and light so they do not show in the final piece. I prefer a size .005 to .007 lead in a mechanical pencil to draw lines of consistent thickness.

### Scissors

When the excess paper around a shape is just scrap and not part of the finished piece, cutting with scissors is quicker than using a craft knife. It is helpful to have a pair of small detail scissors as well as a larger pair of scissors, depending on what needs to be cut.

Mechanical pencil and scissors

### Adhesives

Many paper adhesives are available today. I use archival glue when working on a final piece. For practice pieces, white glue works well. I also like the adhesive tapes and glue dots available at scrapbooking stores because no drying time is involved when using them. Try different adhesives to see which you prefer.

Assorted adhesives

# Additional Tools and Products

The following tools and products are not required for creating pop-up art but are wonderful for enhancing your creations.

**Rubber Stamps and Inkpads** Rubber stamps are a great way to add artwork to your pop-ups without having to draw the image. Use various techniques to create your own designer paper for pop-ups!

**Embossing Powders and a Heat Tool** Embossing powders add dimension and glitz to the final project. The heat tool is needed to activate the powders. See the manufacturer's instructions for applying and heating the powders you choose.

**Rubber stamps, inkpads, and embossing powders**

**Fibers** Ribbons, fibers, and fabrics can all be added to the paper to embellish the piece. These items are usually added after the pop-up is constructed, and they need to be thin (not bulky) so the pop-up closes properly.

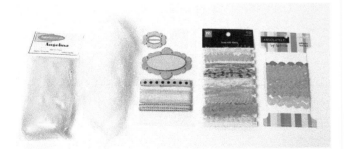

**Different types of fibers**

**Paper Punches and Decorative-Edge Scissors** Using paper punches enables you to add the detailed look of cutwork without having to cut the paper by hand. Many types of paper punches are available today, such as individual paper punches or HyGlo 6-in-1 punches (Sources, page 64) that have a single dial with six different punches. These are fun to use, and the size is just right for smaller projects. Decorative-edge scissors can also be used to add an interesting edge to paper.

**Awl** An awl is a sharp, pointed tool for poking holes in wood, leather, or paper. I prefer an awl to create the holes for fasteners.

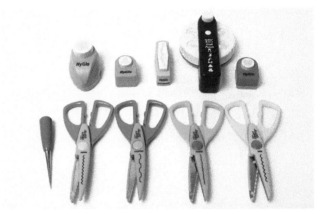

**Paper punches, an awl, and decorative-edge scissors**

**Embellishments** Paper fasteners, eyelets, stickers, charms, and so many more embellishments can be used on pop-ups! Take a trip to the local scrapbooking store; many of the products used in scrapbooking can be used to embellish your pop-ups. Just keep in mind that any embellishments used *inside* the pop-up need to lie nearly flat so they don't prevent the pop-up from closing.

**Assorted embellishments**

# CHAPTER 2

# Creating Pop-Ups

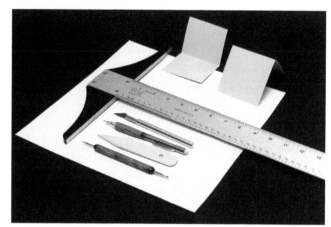

Before venturing down the road of creating pop-ups, read this next chapter. I've provided a list of definitions and how-to instructions on the basic skills—working accurately, drafting, cutting, and gluing—necessary to create a successful pop-up piece.

## POP-UP DEFINITIONS

**Acid Free** Acid-free products have had the acid and lignin removed during the manufacturing process. Acid-free products will last longer than non-acid-free (or non-archival) products and will not yellow and become brittle as quickly.

**Adjacent** Adjacent shapes or lines are placed next to each other.

**Angle** The space between straight lines that meet at a common point.

An angle

**Archival Quality** Archival-quality materials have undergone laboratory testing to determine that their acidic and buffered content is within safe levels and that they will not yellow and age as quickly as non-archival products.

**Armature** A paper framework that supports the pop-up.

**Backer Card** The paper piece to which a pop-up is attached.

**Centerline** The fold across the center of the card.

**Crease Line** A drawn line to be creased for a fold.

**Cut Line** A drawn line to be cut with a craft knife. Cut lines in the instructions in this book are represented with dashed lines.

**Fold** An edge where the paper bends. See Mountain Fold and Valley Fold.

**Glue Point** The exact point where the glue is placed to attach pieces of paper to each other.

**Horizontal Line** A line that goes across the paper from left to right.

**Mountain Fold** A crease line that folds **up** to form a mountain. Mountain folds in the instructions in this book are represented with purple lines.

Mountain fold

**Page Position** The point on the backer card where the pop-up is attached.

**Parallel Lines** Equidistant lines extending in the same direction that will never intersect.

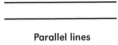

**Parallel lines**

**Perpendicular Lines** Lines that extend at a right angle from each other.

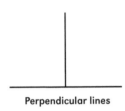

**Perpendicular lines**

**Pop-Up** A collapsible dimensional structure made from paper.

**Score Line** An indentation made in the paper with a ruler and a creasing tool to help the paper fold straight on the line. Score lines in the instructions in this book are represented with orange lines.

**Slot** A cut in the paper where a tab will be inserted.

**Tab** An area that is used to attach a pop-up to another piece of paper, usually by insertion of the tab into a slot.

**Valley Fold** A crease line that folds **down** to form a valley. Valley folds are represented in the instructions in this book with green lines.

**Valley fold**

**Vertical Line** A line that runs down the paper from top to bottom.

# MEASURE AND MARK

Important steps in creating a pop-up piece are drafting (measuring and marking) and cutting. Errors made on either of these steps will prevent the pop-up from working correctly. In this section, I present a general overview on how to draft and cut the lines in a pop-up. You'll use these same techniques whenever you draft lines for pop-ups, but the example shows how to draft a centerline.

A ruler will work perfectly well for creating pop-ups. (I prefer a cork-backed metal ruler—the cork keeps the ruler from sliding, and the metal edge won't get nicked by the craft knife.) However, a T-square (available at craft stores) can make drawing straight lines even easier, in my opinion.

## Draw a Centerline With a Ruler

**1.** Measure up from the short bottom edge of the backer card to a point halfway up the long edges.

**2.** Pencil a dot on each long edge, and use a ruler and a pencil to draw a light line across the width of the card to connect the dots.

Always measure from the bottom, on both edges of the paper, and mark the line's beginning and ending dots. This is the only way to ensure that both points are equidistant from the bottom.

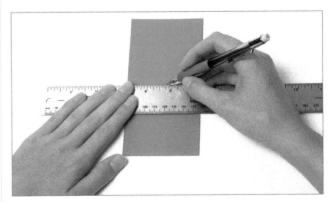

**Drawing a centerline with a ruler**

## Draw a Centerline With a T-square

**1.** Measure up from the short bottom edge of the backer card to a point halfway up the right long edge and pencil a dot at that point.

**2.** Place the T-square on the backer card with the top of the T-square aligned with the left long edge of the paper and the straight edge of the T-square aligned on the halfway dot. Pencil a light line along the straight edge.

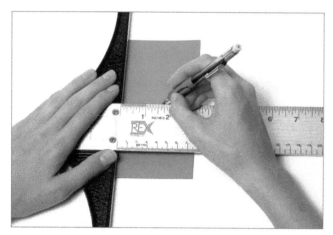

**Drawing a centerline with a T-square**

## Score Lines

All pop-up pieces have lines that need to be scored so the paper will fold straight. I recommend two types of creasing tools: a ball stylus tool and a bone folder. Both tools will crease lines; which one you use is up to you. (However, keep in mind that you can also use a bone folder to press your paper folds shut.)

**1.** Pencil the score line on a piece of paper.

**2.** Put the paper on a flat surface with the line to be scored running vertically.

**3.** Place a cork-backed metal ruler on top of the paper just to the left of the penciled line (or to the right of the line if you are left-handed).

**4.** Place your subordinate hand's index finger and thumb on the center of the ruler. Rest this hand on the tabletop. (Your **subordinate hand** is the opposite of your **dominant hand**—it's your left hand if you are right-handed, and vice versa.)

**5.** Hold the creasing tool in your dominant hand, like a pencil. Place the creasing tool against the ruler at the top of the line (farthest from you).

**6.** Gently and firmly pull the creasing tool toward you against the ruler edge.

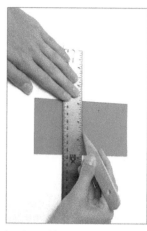

Scoring with a ball stylus tool          Scoring with a point turner

## Create Tabs

On many of the multi-sheet projects in this book, the pop-up pieces require tabs to attach the pieces to the backer card. Here are the basic steps for drafting a tab.

**1.** Pencil a 2˝ square on a practice piece of paper.

**2.** From the bottom line of the square, measure ½˝ down from each corner and pencil a dot.

**3.** With a ruler and pencil, draw a light line under the square, connecting the 2 dots.

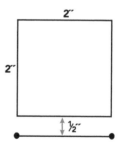

**4.** Pencil a line extending at a 45° angle from a bottom corner to the ½˝ line. Repeat on the other bottom corner.

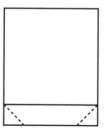

**5.** Cut the square and resulting angles to create the tab.

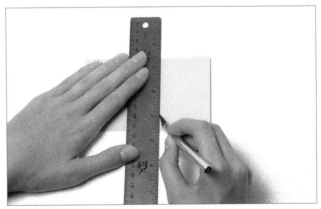

# POP-UP LINE KEY

This key specifies how the various types of lines and folds in the pop-up instructions are represented. Please refer to the key when assembling the pop-ups in this book.

| | |
|---|---|
| **Cut line** | — — — — — — |
| **Score line** | ———————— |
| **Mountain fold** | ———————— |
| **Valley fold** | ———————— |

# CUT WITH A CRAFT KNIFE

A craft knife is a razor blade on a handle; it's a very sharp tool that should be handled with respect. Always be sure your craft knife has a sharp blade in it.

**1.** Draw a practice line on a piece of paper. Place the paper on a self-healing mat with the line running vertically.

**2.** Place a cork-backed metal ruler just to the left of the drawn line (to the right of the drawn line if you are left-handed).

**3.** Place your subordinate hand's index finger and thumb on top of the ruler in the center. Rest this hand on the tabletop. (Your **subordinate hand** is the opposite of your **dominant hand**—it's your left if you are right-handed, and vice versa.)

**4.** Hold the craft knife in your dominant hand, like a pencil. Place the knife against the ruler at the top of the line.

**5.** Stand to the subordinate side of the line and gently but firmly pull the knife toward you down the line, against the ruler's edge.

Cutting a line with a craft knife

# POP-UP FOLDS

Two types of folds are involved in making pop-up pieces: **mountain folds** (represented by purple lines) and **valley folds** (represented by green lines).

Mountain fold        Valley fold

The pop-up techniques in this book start with the mountain folds. Many of the valley folds occur as the mountain folds are creased. Any valley folds not creased when making the mountain folds are folded next.

# APPLYING GLUE

Many adhesives are available on the market. Always refer to the manufacturer's instructions on how to apply the adhesives. I'm going to show you a general method for applying glue to the paper when making pop-ups. The glue has to be spread thin so it doesn't warp the paper or ooze out when the papers being glued are pressed together!

**1.** Place a small dot (or dots) of glue at the glue point.

**Apply small dots of glue.**

**2.** Spread the glue into a thin layer with your finger or the edge of a toothpick before pressing the paper to another surface.

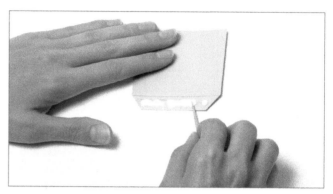

**Spread the glue into a thin layer.**

 tip

*Those phony credit cards you receive in the mail are excellent for spreading glue!*

Now we are ready to move on to making some pop-up art! Refer back to this chapter as you go through the book to get answers to basic questions, to check the definition of a term, or to check the Pop-Up Line Key (page 13).

tip

*Create one of each pop-up described and put the completed pieces in a blank book to create a pop-up sample book for future reference!*

**Pop-up sample books**

# CHAPTER 3

# Simple 90° Pop-Ups

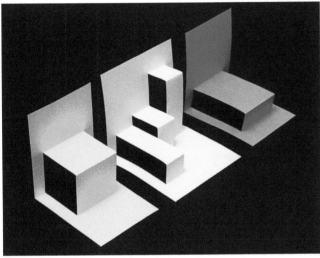

These simple pop-up techniques are the easiest to learn and are great practice for pop-up techniques, such as cutting, creasing, and gluing the pieces together.

## Materials

- Basic tools (see pages 7–9)
- 3″ × 8″ piece of pop-up paper

## Assembly

**1.** On the back of the 3″ × 8″ pop-up paper, measure halfway up from the short bottom edge and pencil a dot on each long edge. Lightly pencil a line from dot to dot across the width of the paper to create the centerline.

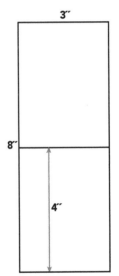

## 90° EQUAL PARALLEL POP-UP

This pop-up can be done as a single-sheet or multi-sheet pop-up. In a single-sheet pop-up, the pop-up and the background are cut from a single piece of paper. The pop-up piece can stand alone or be covered by a backer card. A multi-sheet pop-up is made from individual pieces of paper that are folded and glued in place on a backer card. Each technique creates a different look, and how you are using the pop-up or how you are embellishing it will determine which technique to use.

### Single Sheet

This is the simplest type of 90° pop-up. The top line, centerline, and bottom line are parallel to one another, and the background centerline and the pop-up centerline are one and the same. This type of pop-up is called "equal" because the top and bottom lines are an equal distance from the centerline.

**tip**

*90° pop-ups work when the piece is opened at a right angle. If the piece is opened wider than 90°, the pop-up will fold down flat, or in some cases, the pop-up may even tear if overextended.*

**2.** Measure ½″ in from each long edge on the drawn centerline and pencil a dot.

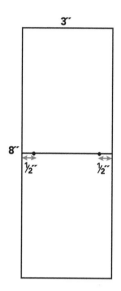

**3.** Measure 2″ up from the left centerline dot and pencil a dot. Measure 2″ down from the left centerline dot and pencil another dot. Lightly pencil a line between the dots to create the left sideline.

**4.** Repeat Step 3 on the right side of the centerline to create the right sideline.

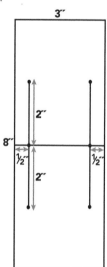

**5.** Lightly pencil a line between the tops of the pop-up sidelines to create the top horizontal line. Repeat to create the bottom horizontal line. The rectangle drawn on the page is the pop-up shape; the paper outside the rectangle is the background.

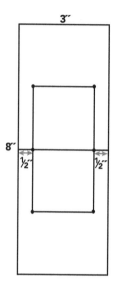

**6.** Score the drawn horizontal lines with a creasing tool.

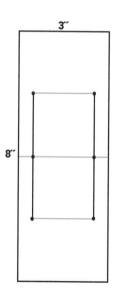

**7.** With a craft knife and metal ruler, cut on the drawn vertical sidelines to make the pop-up side slits. Now we are ready to make the piece three-dimensional!

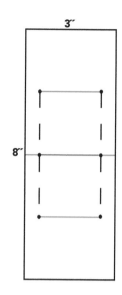

**8.** Turn the pop-up paper over to the front. Slide one of your middle fingers into each of the pop-up side slits. Place your index fingers above the centerline and your thumbs below the centerline.

**9.** Gently pull the center cut area toward you. It will want to fold on the scored centerline. Crease a mountain fold on the centerline within the drawn rectangle and valley folds on the background centerline and the top and bottom horizontal pop-up lines.

**10.** Fold the pop-up completely closed and press it shut on a flat surface to ensure straight and tight folds. Reopen the pop-up to see the finished single-sheet 90° Equal Parallel Pop-Up!

## Multi-Sheet

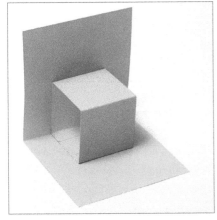

The multi-sheet version of this pop-up works the same as the single-sheet version but is assembled with multiple sheets of paper. Making this pop-up with more sheets allows you to add more colors!

### Materials

- Basic tools (see pages 7–9)
- 2″ × 8½″ piece of pop-up paper
- 4″ × 8″ piece of backer card
- Adhesive

### Assembly

**1.** On the back of the 2″ × 8½″ pop-up paper, measure and mark the following points on each long edge, from left to right: 2″, 4″, 6″, and 8″. Lightly pencil a line across the width of the paper at each set of marks.

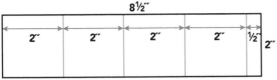

**2.** Score the drawn lines with a creasing tool.

**3.** Turn the pop-up paper over to the front and mountain fold each scored line to create a 2″ square box. Apply glue to the ½″ tab and glue the tab to the inside of the adjacent 2″ edge. Set aside.

**4.** On the back of the 4″ × 8″ backer card, measure halfway up from the short bottom edge and pencil a dot on each long edge. Lightly pencil a line from dot to dot across the width of the backer card to create the centerline.

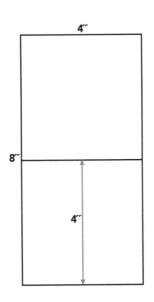

**5.** Score the centerline with a creasing tool. Turn the backer card over to the front and fold it in half on the scored line.

**6.** Open the backer card. Measure 1″ in from each long edge on the centerline and pencil a dot inside the backer card to mark the page position for the pop-up.

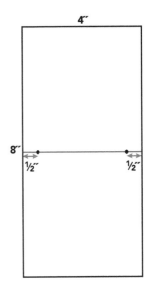

**7.** Orient the pop-up square box from Step 3 so the glued tab is in the upper back corner. Apply glue to the square on top of the box. Turn the box over and center it on the page position marked on the backer card's centerline. Press the box onto the top half of the backer card, so that the back edge of the box is tight against the backer card's centerline fold. Let the glue dry.

**8.** Push the pop-up square box flat against the backer card. Apply glue to the square that will be against the backer card. Close the backer card down on top of the pop-up. Let the glue dry.

**9.** Once the glue has dried, open the pop-up to see the finished multi-sheet 90° Equal Parallel Pop-Up!

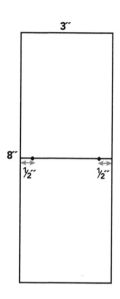

# 90° UNEQUAL PARALLEL POP-UP

## Single Sheet

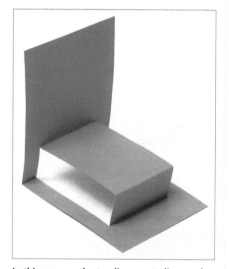

In this pop-up, the top line, centerline, and bottom line are parallel to one another. This type of pop-up is called "unequal" because the top and bottom lines are not an equal distance from the centerline.

## Materials

- Basic tools (see pages 7–9)
- 3″ × 8″ piece of pop-up paper

## Assembly

**1.** On the back of the 3″ × 8″ pop-up paper, measure halfway up from the short bottom edge and pencil a dot on each long edge. Lightly pencil a line from dot to dot across the width of the paper to create the centerline.

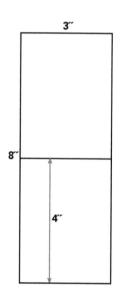

**2.** Measure ½″ in from each long edge on the drawn centerline and pencil a dot.

**3.** Measure 2″ up from the left centerline dot and pencil another dot. Measure 3″ up from the left centerline dot and pencil another dot. Measure 1″ down from the left centerline dot and pencil another dot. Lightly pencil a line between the dots to create the left sideline.

**4.** Repeat Step 3 on the right side of the centerline to create the right sideline.

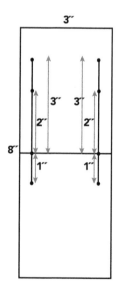

**5.** Lightly pencil horizontal lines between the 2 sidelines to connect the dots 2″ and 3″ above the centerline and the dots 1″ below the centerline. The rectangle drawn on the page is the pop-up shape—the paper outside the rectangle is the background. Erase the background centerline that is *inside* the drawn rectangle.

6. Score the drawn horizontal lines with a creasing tool. Be sure to score the background centerline only *outside* the pop-up rectangle.

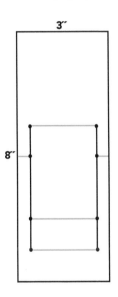

7. With a craft knife and metal ruler, cut on the drawn vertical side-lines to make the pop-up side slits. Now we are ready to make the piece three-dimensional!

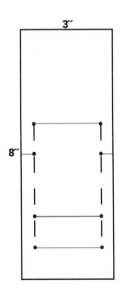

8. Turn the pop-up paper over to the front. Slide one of your middle fingers into each of the pop-up side slits. Place your index fingers above the pop-up centerline and your thumbs below the pop-up centerline.

9. Gently pull the center cut area toward you. Crease a mountain fold on the pop-up centerline and valley folds on the background centerline and on the top and bottom horizontal pop-up lines.

10. Fold the pop-up completely closed and press it down on a flat surface to ensure straight and tight folds. Reopen the pop-up to see the finished single-sheet 90° Unequal Parallel Pop-Up!

## Multi-Sheet

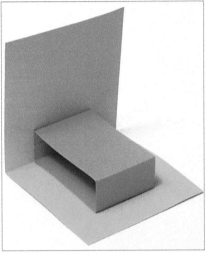

The multi-sheet version of this pop-up works the same as the single-sheet version but is assembled with multiple sheets of paper. Making this pop-up with multiple sheets allows you to add more colors.

### Materials

- Basic tools (see pages 7–9)
- 2″ × 8½″ piece of pop-up paper
- 4″ × 8″ piece of backer card
- Adhesive

### Assembly

1. On the back of the 2″ × 8½″ pop-up paper, measure and mark the following points on each long edge, from left to right: 1″, 4″, 5″, and 8″. Lightly pencil a line across the width of the paper at each set of marks. Score the drawn lines with a creasing tool.

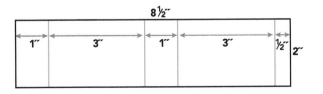

**2.** Turn the pop-up paper over to the front and mountain fold each scored line to create a 1″ × 3″ rectangle box. Apply glue to the ½″ tab and glue the tab to the inside of the adjacent 1″ edge of the box. Set aside.

**3.** On the back of the 4″ × 8″ backer card, measure halfway up from the short bottom edge and pencil a dot on each long edge. Lightly pencil a line from dot to dot across the width of the backer card to create the centerline. Score the centerline with a creasing tool.

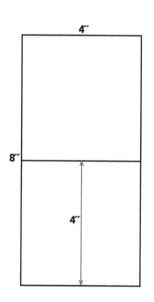

**4.** Turn the backer card to the front and fold it in half on the scored line.

**5.** Open the backer card. Measure 1″ in from each long edge on the centerline and pencil a dot inside the backer card to mark the page position for the pop-up.

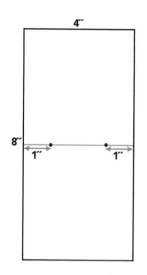

**6.** Orient the pop-up rectangle box from Step 3 so the glued tab is in the upper back corner. Apply glue to the top of the 1″ side of the box.

**7.** Turn the box over and center it on the page position on the backer card's centerline. Press the box to the bottom half of the backer card, so that the back edge of the box is tight against the backer card's centerline fold. Let the glue dry.

**8.** Push the box down flat against the bottom of the backer card. Apply glue to the 2″ × 3″ rectangle. Close the backer card down on top of the pop-up. Let the glue dry.

**9.** Once the glue has dried, turn it around and open the pop-up to see the finished multi-sheet 90° Unequal Parallel Pop-Up!

# 90° EQUAL AND UNEQUAL PARALLEL POP-UP

## Single Sheet

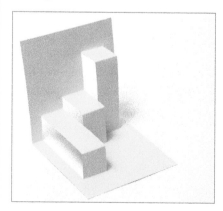

This project contains both equal and unequal parallel pop-ups on one sheet of paper. The challenge in making pop-ups is to mark everything accurately and to fold each crease line carefully without damaging the remaining piece of paper. This example uses three pop-ups.

### Materials

- Basic tools (see pages 7–9)
- 4″ × 8″ piece of pop-up paper

## Assembly

1. On the back of the 4″ × 8″ pop-up paper, measure halfway up from the short bottom edge and pencil a dot on each long edge. Lightly pencil a line from dot to dot across the width of the paper to create the centerline.

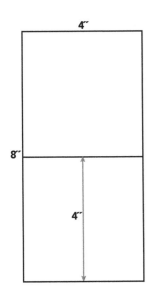

2. Measure and mark the following points on the drawn centerline, from right to left: ½″, 1½″, 2½″, and 3½″.

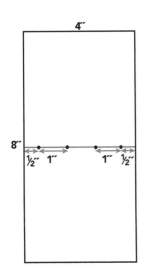

3. **For the first pop-up:** Measure 2″ up from the leftmost dot on the centerline and pencil a second dot. Measure 3″ up from leftmost dot on the centerline and pencil a third dot. Measure 1″ down from leftmost dot on the centerline and pencil a fourth dot. Lightly pencil a line between the dots to create the first pop-up's left sideline.

4. Repeat Step 3 with the second dot from the left to create the first pop-up's right sideline.

5. Pencil a horizontal line connecting the 1″ dots to create the bottom horizontal line. Pencil a second line connecting the 2″ dots to create the center horizontal line and a third line connecting the 3″ dots to create the top horizontal line. Erase the background centerline that is *inside* the drawn rectangle.

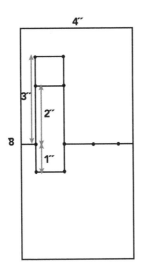

6. **For the second pop-up:** Moving to the rightmost dot on the centerline, measure 1″ up and pencil a second dot. Measure 2″ down from the centerline and pencil a third dot. Measure 3″ down from the centerline and pencil a fourth dot. Lightly pencil a line between the dots to create the second pop-up's right sideline.

7. Repeat Step 5 with the second dot from the right to create the second pop-up's left sideline.

8. Pencil a horizontal line connecting the 1″ dots to create the top horizontal line. Pencil a second line connecting the 2″ dots to create the centerline and a third line connecting the 3″ dots to create the bottom horizontal line. Erase the background centerline that is *inside* the drawn rectangle.

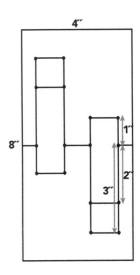

9. **For the third pop-up:** The third pop-up shares its left sideline with the first pop-up's right sideline. On this sideline, measure 2″ up from the centerline and pencil a dot. Measure 2″ down from the centerline and pencil another dot.

10. The third pop-up shares its right sideline with the second pop-up's left sideline. On this sideline, measure 2″ up from the centerline and pencil a dot. Measure 2″ down from the centerline and pencil another dot. Pencil a horizontal line connecting the 2 top dots. Pencil another line connecting the 2 bottom dots.

**11.** Score the drawn horizontal lines with a creasing tool.

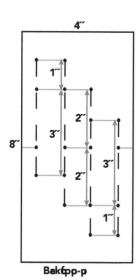

**Bakfpp-p**

**12.** With a craft knife and metal ruler, cut on all the drawn vertical sidelines to create the pop-up side slits. Turn the pop-up paper over to the front. Now we are ready to make the piece three-dimensional!

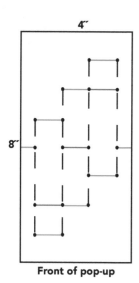

**Front of pop-up**

**13.** Slide one of your middle fingers into each of the 2 leftmost pop-up side slits. Place your index fingers above the pop-up centerline and your thumbs below the pop-up centerline.

**14.** Gently pull the center cut area of the first pop-up toward you. Crease a mountain fold on the pop-up center-line. Crease valley folds on the top and bottom horizontal pop-up lines of the first pop-up.

**15.** Repeat Steps 13 and 14 with the remaining 2 pop-ups. Gently crease a valley fold on the background centerline.

**16.** Fold the pop-up completely closed and press it down on a flat surface to ensure straight and tight folds. Reopen the pop-up to see the finished single-sheet 90° Equal and Unequal Parallel Pop-Up!

## Multi-Sheet

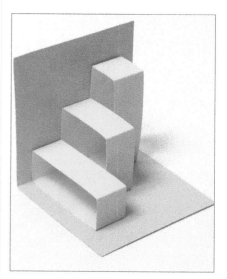

Create each of the pop-up boxes as shown in the multi-sheet 90° Equal Parallel Pop-Up (pages 17–19) and the multi-sheet 90° Unequal Parallel Pop-Up (pages 19–20) and glue them onto the same backer card.

**Tip**

*A multi-sheet 90° Equal and Unequal Parallel Pop-Up is much easier to create than the single-sheet version, but the single-sheet version has a more elegant look.*

# ntermediate 90° Pop-Ups

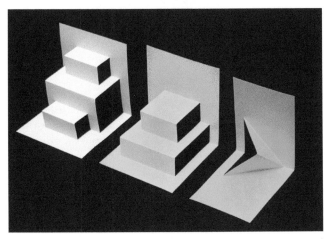

These pop-up pieces also work only when opened at a 90° angle, and they are a little more challenging than the simple 90° pop-ups (owing to the number of folds and cuts). Many of these pieces build on the pop-up techniques covered in Chapter 3.

## 90° EQUAL ANGLE POP-UP

### Single Sheet

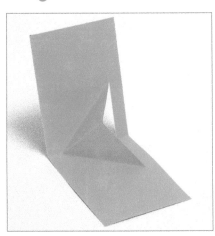

Angles can be tricky to work with, but this angled pop-up is simple to create. It is made by drawing angles from the centerline to marks above and below the centerline.

### Materials

- Basic tools (see pages 7–9)
- 3″ × 8″ piece of pop-up paper

### Assembly

**1.** On the back of the 3″ × 8″ pop-up paper, measure halfway up from the short bottom edge and pencil a dot on each long edge. Lightly pencil a line from dot to dot across the width of the paper to create the centerline.

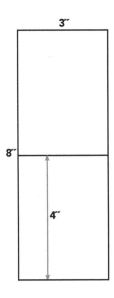

**2.** Measure ½″ in from each long edge on the drawn centerline and pencil a dot.

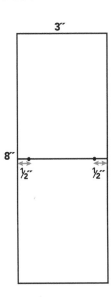

**3.** Measure 2″ up from the right dot on the centerline and pencil a second dot. Measure 2″ down and pencil a third dot. Lightly pencil a line between the dots to create the right sideline.

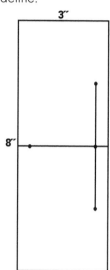

**4.** With a craft knife and a metal ruler, cut on the drawn right sideline.

**5.** From the left centerline dot, lightly pencil a line to the top 2″ dot on the right to create the top angle. From the left centerline dot, lightly pencil a line to the bottom 2″ dot on the right to create the bottom angle.

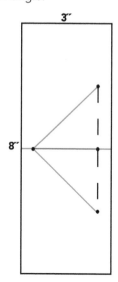

**6.** With a creasing tool, score the drawn centerline across the entire width of the paper and score the 2 drawn angle lines.

**7.** Turn the pop-up paper over to the front. Slide your middle finger into the pop-up side slit. Place your index finger above the pop-up centerline and your thumb below the pop-up centerline.

**8.** Gently pull the angle toward you. Crease a mountain fold on the pop-up centerline and valley folds on the top and bottom angle lines as well as on the background centerline.

**9.** Close the pop-up completely and press it on a flat surface to ensure straight and tight folds. Reopen the pop-up to see the 90° Equal Angle Pop-Up!

# Multi-Sheet

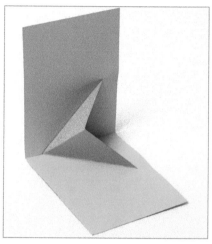

The 90° Equal Angle Pop-Up is usually done with multiple sheets rather than a single sheet and can be used to create a mouth on a pop-up character. Using multiple sheets allows you to make the mouth a different color than the card background.

## Materials

- Basic tools (see pages 7–9)
- 2″ × 4″ piece of pop-up paper
- 3″ × 8″ piece of backer card
- Adhesive

## Assembly

**1.** On the back of the 2″ × 4″ pop-up paper, measure halfway up from the short bottom edge and pencil a dot on each long edge. Lightly pencil a line from dot to dot across the width of the paper to create the centerline.

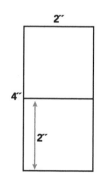

**2.** Lightly pencil a line from the left end of the centerline to the upper right corner of the pop-up paper. Lightly pencil another line from the left end of the centerline to the lower right corner.

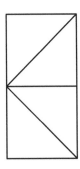

**3.** Following the general instructions for creating tabs (pages 12–13), draft 2 tabs on the pop-up, as indicated in the illustration. Cut out the pop-up angle.

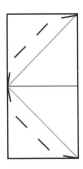

**4.** With a creasing tool, score the drawn centerline across the entire width of the paper and score the 2 drawn angle lines. Crease a mountain fold on the pop-up centerline and crease valley folds at the tabs.

**5.** On the back of the 3″ × 8″ backer card, measure halfway up from the short bottom edge and pencil a dot on each long edge. Lightly pencil a line from dot to dot, across the width of the backer card, to create the centerline. Score the centerline with a creasing tool.

**6.** Place the flat pop-up angle on top of the backer card, aligning the centerlines. Mark the sides of the tabs with dots on the backer card; then remove the pop-up piece.

**7.** On the backer card, lightly pencil a line from dot to dot above the centerline, to mark where the top tab fits. Repeat with the dots below the centerline. With a craft knife, cut on the drawn lines to create slots in the backer card for the pop-up tabs.

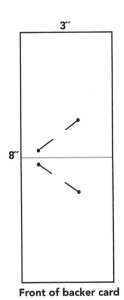

3″

8″

**Front of backer card**

**8.** Turn the backer card over to the front and fold it in half on the scored line.

**9.** Open the backer card. Gently slide the pop-up angle tabs into the cut slits on the backer card.

**10.** Turn the entire piece over. Fold each tab flush with the backer card, keeping the angle tab at a valley fold. Glue the tabs to the back of the backer card. Let the glue dry.

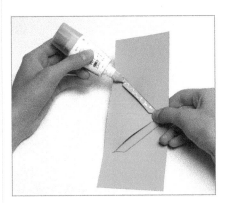

**11.** Once the glue dries, push the pop-up down flat to create tight folds. Reopen the pop-up to see the finished multi-sheet 90° Equal Angle Pop-Up!

# 90° EQUAL GENERATIONS POP-UP

## Single Sheet

To create this pop-up, draft a 90° Equal Parallel Pop-Up and then add another pop-up that overlaps the first. The top or bottom valley fold on the first pop-up piece becomes the centerline of the second pop-up piece. You can overlap pop-ups as many times as the paper size allows.

### Materials

- Basic tools (see pages 7–9)
- 4″ × 8″ piece of pop-up paper

### Assembly

**1.** On the back of the 4″ × 8″ pop-up paper, measure halfway up from the short bottom edge and pencil a dot on each long edge. Lightly pencil a line from dot to dot across the width of the paper to create the centerline. Score the centerline with a creasing tool.

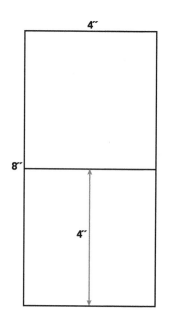

**2.** Measure ½″ in from each long edge on the drawn centerline and pencil a dot.

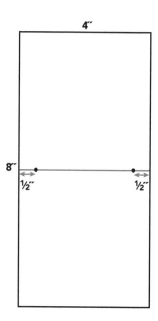

**3.** Measure 2″ up from the left centerline dot and pencil another dot. Measure 2″ down from the left centerline dot and pencil a third

dot. Lightly pencil a line between the dots to create the left sideline.

**4.** Repeat Step 3 on the right side of the centerline to create the right sideline.

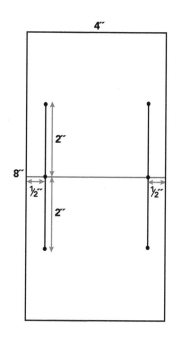

**5.** Lightly pencil a line between the tops of the pop-up sidelines to create the top horizontal line. Repeat to create the bottom horizontal line. The rectangle drawn on the page is the first pop-up shape.

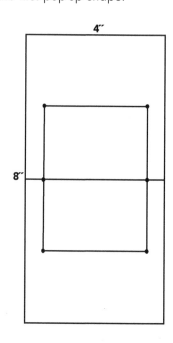

**6.** On the top horizontal line, measure ½″ in from each of the drawn sidelines and pencil a dot. Using the top horizontal line as the new centerline, measure 1″ up from the left dot and pencil another dot. Then measure 1″ down and pencil another dot. Lightly pencil a line connecting the dots. Repeat with the right side dot.

**7.** Lightly pencil a horizontal line connecting the top 1″ lines. Repeat to connect the bottom 1″ lines. Now you have a large rectangle that is the first pop-up and a smaller rectangle (overlapping the first rectangle) that is the second pop-up.

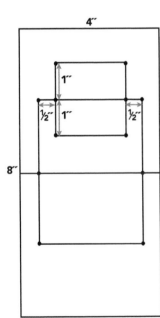

**8.** Repeat Steps 6 and 7 on the bottom horizontal line of the first pop-up to create a third pop-up.

**9.** Score the drawn horizontal lines with a creasing tool.

**10.** With a craft knife and metal ruler, cut on the vertical drawn lines to make the pop-up side slits. Now we are ready to make the piece three-dimensional!

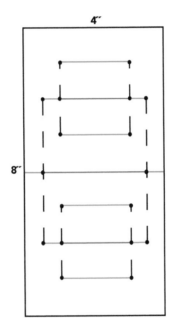

**11.** Turn the pop-up paper over to the front. Slide one of your middle fingers into each of the outer pop-up side slits. Place your index fingers above the first centerline and your thumbs below the centerline.

**12.** Gently pull the center cut area toward you. It will want to fold on the scored centerline. Crease a mountain fold on the centerline. Repeat with the second and third pop-ups, creasing mountain folds on the smaller centerlines. Carefully crease valley folds on the rest of the scored lines.

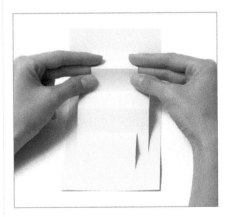

**13.** Close the pop-up completely and press it flat to ensure straight and tight folds. Reopen the pop-up to see the finished 90° Equal Generations Pop-Up. You can leave the pop-up piece as is or add a backer card.

# Multi-Sheet

To create this pop-up, you will make individual paper boxes for each step of the 90° Equal Generations Pop-Up; **and** then you'll glue the cubes on top of each other. Unlike the single-sheet technique, which only uses one sheet for the pop-up, this technique lets you create pop-ups out of several different colors.

## Materials

- Basic tools (see pages 7–9)
- 3″ × 8½″ piece of pop-up paper
- 2 pieces 2″ × 4½″ of pop-up paper
- 4″ × 8″ piece of backer card
- Adhesive

## Assembly

**1.** On the back of the 3″ × 8½″ pop-up paper, measure and mark the following points left to right on each long edge: 2″, 4″, 6″, and 8″. Lightly pencil a line across the width of the paper at each set of marks. Score the drawn lines with a creasing tool.

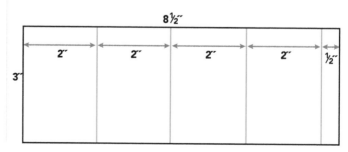

**2.** On the back of both 2″ × 4½″ pop-up papers, measure and mark the following points left to right on each long edge: 1″, 2″, 3″, and 4″. Lightly pencil a line across the width of the papers at each set of marks. Score the drawn lines with a creasing tool.

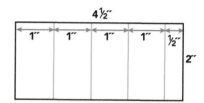

**3.** Turn the pop-up papers over to the front and fold each scored line to create a 2″ box and a pair of 1″ boxes. Apply glue to the ½″ tab on each box and glue the tabs to the inside of the adjacent edges. Set aside.

**4.** On the back of the 4″ × 8″ backer card, measure halfway up from the short bottom edge and pencil a dot on each long edge. Lightly pencil a line from dot to dot across the width of the backer card to create the centerline. Score the centerline with a creasing tool.

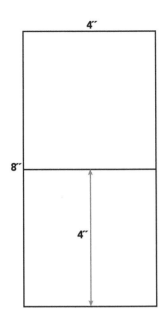

**5.** Turn the backer card over to the front and fold it in half on the scored line. Open the backer card. Measure ½″ in from each 4″ edge on the centerline and pencil a dot to mark the page position for the pop-up.

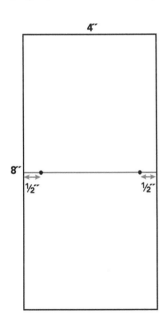

**6.** Orient the 2″ pop-up box from Step 3 so the glued tab is in the

upper front corner. Apply glue to the top of the box. Turn the box over and center it between the dots on the backer card's centerline. Glue the box to the bottom half of the backer card, so that its back edge is tight against the backer card's centerline fold.

**7.** Push the box down flat and apply glue to the left top rectangle. Close the backer card down on top of the pop-up. Let the glue dry.

**8.** Once the glue has dried on the first pop-up piece, open the card. Measure ½″ in from each edge of

the first pop-up along the top line and pencil a dot. Repeat with the bottom line.

**9.** Orient one of the 1″ pop-up boxes from Step 3 so that the glued tab is in the upper front corner. Apply glue to the top of the box. Turn the box over and center it between the top line dots on the first pop-up. Glue the 1″ box to the top of the first pop-up so that the back edge is tight against the backer card. Glue the back edge to the backer card.

**10.** Turn the card around so the 1″ box is on the bottom. Repeat Step 9 with the other 1″ box and the bottom line of the first pop-up. Glue the bottom edge to the backer card.

# 90° UNEQUAL GENERATIONS POP-UP

## Single Sheet

This pop-up is created by drafting a 90° Unequal Parallel Pop-Up and then adding another pop-up that overlaps the first pop-up piece. The top or bottom valley fold on the first pop-up piece becomes the centerline of the second pop-up piece. You can overlap layers as many times as the paper size will allow.

## Materials

- Basic tools (see pages 6-9)
- 4″ × 8″ piece of pop-up paper

## Assembly

**1.** On the back of the 4″ × 8″ pop-up paper, measure halfway up from the short bottom edge and pencil a dot on each long edge. Lightly pencil a line from dot to dot across the width of the paper to create the centerline.

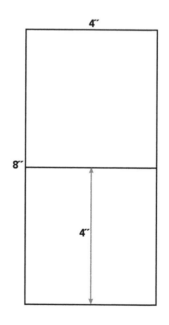

**2.** Measure ½″ in from each long edge on the drawn centerline and pencil a dot.

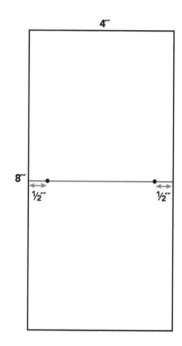

**3.** Measure 2″ down from the left centerline dot and pencil a second dot. Measure 3″ down from the left centerline dot and pencil a third dot. Measure 1″ up from the centerline dot and pencil a fourth dot. Lightly pencil a vertical line through these dots to create the left pop-up sideline.

**4.** Repeat Step 3 on the right side of the centerline to create the right pop-up sideline.

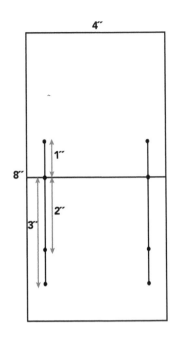

**5.** Lightly pencil a line between the top pop-up sideline dots to create the top horizontal line. Draw a second line between the 2″ dots and a third line between the 3″ dots to create the bottom horizontal line. The rectangle drawn on the page is the first pop-up shape.

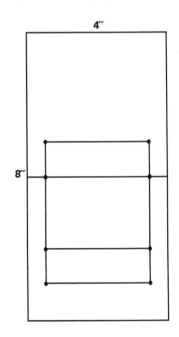

**6.** Measure 1″ in and 1″ down from the left centerline dot and pencil a dot. Measure 1″ in and 2″ up from the left centerline dot and pencil another dot. Lightly pencil a vertical line through these dots to create a second left pop-up sideline. Repeat on the right side of the centerline to create the second right pop-up sideline.

**7.** Lightly pencil a horizontal line connecting the bottom dots. Repeat to connect the top dots. Now you have a large rectangle that is the first pop-up and a smaller rectangle (overlapping the first rectangle) that is the second pop-up. Erase the centerlines in the areas shown in the illustration.

**8.** Score the drawn horizontal lines with a creasing tool.

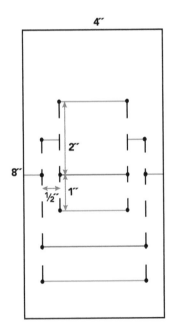

**9.** With a craft knife and ruler, cut on all the vertical drawn lines to make the side slits. Now we are ready to make the piece three-dimensional!

**10.** Turn the pop-up paper over to the front. Slide one of your middle fingers into each of the outer pop-up side slits. Place your index fingers and your thumbs as shown.

**11.** Gently pull the center cut area toward you. Crease a mountain fold. Repeat with the second pop-up. Carefully crease valley folds on the rest of the scored lines.

**12.** Close the pop-up completely and press it flat to ensure straight and tight folds. Reopen the pop-up to see the finished single-sheet 90° Unequal Generations Pop-Up. You can leave the pop-up piece as is or add a backer card.

# Multi-Sheet

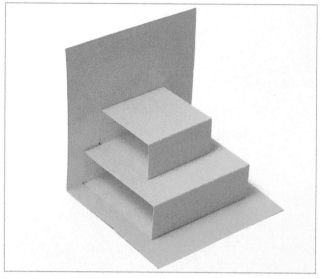

To make this pop-up, you will make individual paper boxes for each step of the Unequal Generations Pop-Up and then glue the cubes on top of each other. Unlike the single-sheet technique, which only uses one sheet for the pop-up, this technique lets you create pop-ups out of several different colors.

## Materials

- Basic tools (see pages 7–9)
- 3″ × 8½″ piece of pop-up paper
- 2″ × 6½″ piece of pop-up paper
- 4″ × 8″ piece of backer card
- Adhesive

## Assembly

1. On the back of the 3″ × 8½″ pop-up paper, measure and mark the following points on each long edge, from left to right: 1″, 4″, 5″, and 8″. Lightly pencil a line across the width of the paper at each set of marks. Score the drawn lines with a creasing tool.

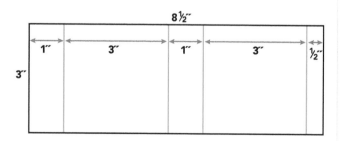

2. On the back of both 2″ × 6½″ pop-up papers, measure and mark the following points on each long edge, from left to right: 1″, 3″, 4″, and 6″. Lightly pencil a line across the width of the papers at each set of marks. Score the drawn lines with a creasing tool.

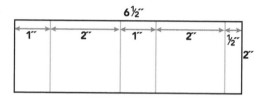

3. Turn the pop-up papers over and fold each crease line to create a large 1″ × 3″ rectangle box and a small 1″ × 2″ rectangle box. Apply glue to the ½″ tabs of both boxes and glue the tabs to the insides of the adjacent edges. Set aside.

4. On the back of the 4″ × 8″ backer card, measure halfway up from the short bottom edge and pencil a dot on each long edge. Lightly pencil a line from dot to dot across the width of the backer card to create the centerline. Score the centerline with a creasing tool.

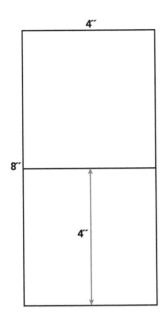

**5.** Turn the backer card over and fold it in half on the scored line. Open the folded backer card. Measure ½″ in from each long edge on the centerline and pencil a dot to mark the page position for the pop-up.

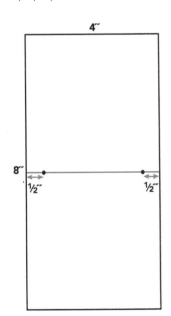

**6.** Orient the large rectangle box from Step 3 so the glued tab is in the upper front corner. Apply glue to the top of the box. Turn the box over and center it between the dots on the backer card's centerline, so that its back edge is tight against the backer card's centerline fold and the glue is against the bottom section of the backing card. Press the box into place to ensure that the glue bonds.

**7.** Push the box flat and apply glue to the top rectangle section. Close the backer card down on the pop-up. Let the glue dry.

**8.** Once the glue has dried on the first pop-up piece, open the card. Measure ½″ in from each side of the first pop-up along the top line and pencil a dot.

**9.** Orient the small rectangle box from Step 3 so the glued tab is in the upper front corner. Apply glue to the top of the small rectangle box. Turn the small rectangle box over and center it between the top line dots on the first pop-up. Glue the small box to the top of the large box, so that the back edge of the former is tight against the backer card. Push the rectangle down to ensure that the glue bonds. Press the pop-up rectangle shut, apply glue to the small top rectangle section, and close the backer card. Let the glue dry.

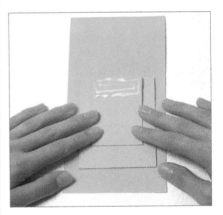

**10.** Reopen the pop-up to see the finished multi-sheet 90° Unequal Generations Pop-Up!

# CHAPTER 5

# 180° Pop-Ups

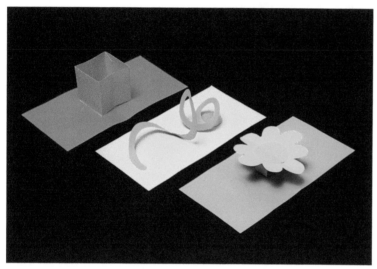

Unlike 90° pop-ups, 180° pop-ups usually involve two sheets of paper. Once the 180° pop-up is constructed, any of the 90° pop-ups can be added to it to make it look much more complicated.

## 180° BOX POP-UP

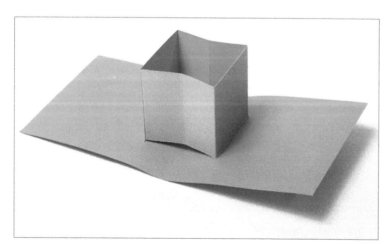

This technique involves creating a three-dimensional box pop-up in the center of the card. This great pop-up can be used in many ways. Once you get the hang of it, you can manipulate it into all kinds of things, such as a house, a photo cube, or an armature to add other artwork. (I varied the top of the box sides to create the Pop-Up House note cards on page 49.)

### Materials

- Basic tools (see pages 7–9)
- 4″ × 8″ piece of backer card
- 2½″ × 8½″ piece of pop-up paper
- Adhesive

### Assembly

**1.** On the back of the 4″ × 8″ backer card, measure halfway up from the short bottom edge and pencil a dot on each long edge. Lightly pencil a line from dot to dot across the width of the card to create the centerline. Score the centerline with a creasing tool.

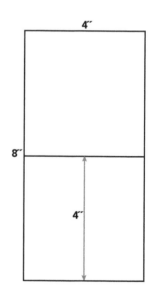

2. Turn the backer card over to the front and fold it in half on the scored line.

3. Open the backer card. Measure 1″ from each long edge on the centerline and pencil a dot.

4. Measure 1″ up from the right centerline dot and pencil a second dot. Measure 1″ down from the center-line dot and pencil a third dot. Do the same for the left centerline dot. Lightly pencil a line between the top 2 dots and another line between the bottom 2 dots.

5. Cut a slit on these 2 drawn lines with a craft knife. Set aside.

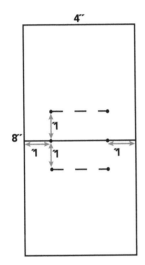

6. On the back of the 2½″ × 8½″ pop-up paper, measure and mark the following points on each long edge, from left to right: 2″, 3″, 4″, 6″, 7″, and 8″. Lightly pencil a line across the width of the paper at each set of marks. Score the drawn lines with a creasing tool.

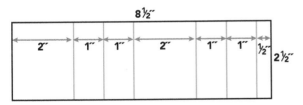

7. Measure ½″ up from the bottom long edge and pencil a dot on each short edge. Lightly pencil a line from dot to dot across the bottom of the paper. Following the general instructions for creating tabs (pages 12–13), draft 2 tabs on the bottom of the pop-up and on the end that is marked with the ½″ segment.

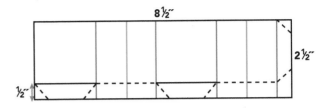

8. Cut out the tabs and score the rest of the drawn lines with a creasing tool.

9. Turn the pop-up paper over to the front and fold it into a 2″ box. Glue the ½″ side tab inside the adjacent edge to form a box with 2 bottom tabs.

10. Fold the 2 bottom tabs out. Place the 2″ pop-up box on the front of the backer card. Slide one pop-up tab into each of the cut slits. Turn the entire piece over and glue the tabs in place. Let the glue dry.

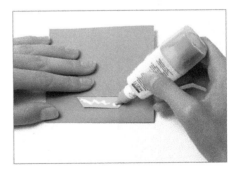

11. Gently fold the pop-up card closed and press it down to ensure straight and tight folds. Reopen the pop-up to see the 180° Box Pop-Up!

# 180° ANGLED BOX POP-UP

This is another way to create a box pop-up. The difference is that this one is on point. Because it is on an angle, side creases are not necessary. Elimination of the side creases produces a cleaner-looking square. However, the angle of the pop-up requires a larger backer card.

## Materials

- Basic tools (see pages 7–9)
- 5″ × 9″ piece of backer card
- 2½″ × 8½″ piece of pop-up paper
- Adhesive

## Assembly

**1.** On the back of the 5″ × 9″ backer card, measure halfway up from the short bottom edge and pencil a dot on each long edge. Lightly pencil a line from dot to dot across the width of the backer card to create the centerline. Score the centerline with a creasing tool.

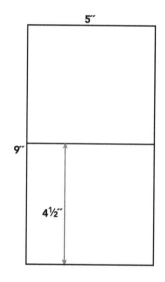

**2.** Turn the backer card over and fold it in half on the scored line.

**3.** Open the backer card. On the front of the backer card, measure 1½″ in from one edge and pencil a dot on the centerline. Measure and mark a second dot at 3″. From the second dot, measure 1½″ above the centerline and pencil a third dot, and then measure 1½″ below the centerline and pencil a fourth dot.

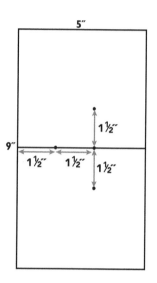

**4.** Lightly pencil a diagonal line from the first 1½″ dot on the center-line to the **third** dot **above** the centerline. Lightly pencil another diagonal line from the first dot on the centerline to the **fourth** dot **below** the centerline.

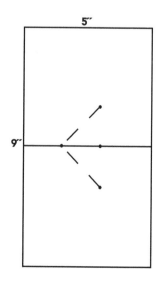

**5.** On the back of the 2½″ × 8½″ pop-up paper, measure and mark the following points on each long edge, from left to right: 2″, 4″ 6″, and 8″. Lightly pencil a line across the width of the paper at each set of marks. Score the drawn lines with a creasing tool.

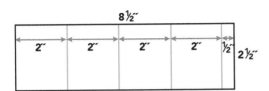

**6.** Measure ½″ up from the bottom long edge and pencil a dot on each short edge. Lightly pencil a line from dot to dot across the bottom of the paper. Following the general directions for creating tabs (page 12), draft 2 tabs on both the bottom of the pop-up and on the end with the drawn ½″ segment.

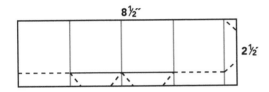

**7.** Cut out the tabs and score the rest of the drawn lines with a creasing tool.

**8.** Turn the pop-up paper over to the front and fold it into a 2″ box. Glue the ½″ side tab inside the adjacent edge to form a box with 2 bottom tabs.

**9.** Fold the 2 bottom tabs out. Place the pop-up box onto the front of the backer card. Align the fold line between each tab and the edge with each of the 2 drawn 45° diagonal lines on the backer card. Pencil a dot where the tabs end on the drawn line.

**10.** Cut slits on each of the diagonal lines with a craft knife. Erase all the pencil lines on the backer card.

**11.** Slide a pop-up tab into each of the slits. Turn the entire piece over and glue the tabs in place. Let the glue dry.

**12.** Gently fold the pop-up card closed and press it down to ensure straight and tight folds. Reopen the pop-up to see the 180° Angle Box Pop-Up!

# 180° CUBE POP-UP

This technique allows you to create a closed pop-up box in the center of a card.

## Materials

- Basic tools (see pages 7–9)
- 4″ × 8″ piece of backer card
- 5″ × 8½″ piece of pop-up paper
- Adhesive

## Assembly

**1.** On the back of the 4″ × 8″ backer card, measure halfway up from the short bottom edge and pencil a dot on each long edge. Lightly pencil a line from dot to dot across the width of the backer card to create the centerline. Score the centerline with a creasing tool.

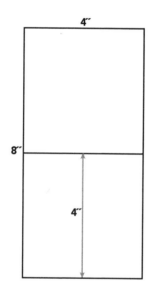

**2.** Turn the backer card over to the front and fold it in half on the scored line.

**3.** Open the backer card. Measure 1″ in from each long edge on the centerline and pencil a dot.

**4.** Measure 1″ up and 1″ down from each centerline dot and pencil a dot. Lightly pencil a line between the top dots and another between the bottom dots.

**5.** Cut a slit on each of the 2 drawn lines with a craft knife. Set aside.

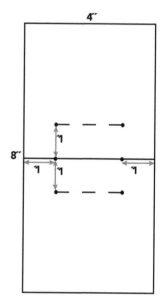

**6.** On the back of the 5″ × 8½″ pop-up paper, measure and mark the following points on each long edge, from left to right: 2″, 3″, 4″ 6″, 7″, and 8″. Lightly pencil a line across the width of the paper at each set of marks. Score the drawn lines with a creasing tool.

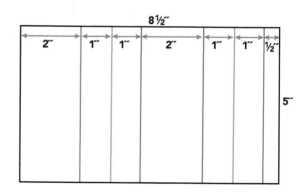

7. Measure and mark the following points from left to right on each short edge: ½″, 2½″, and 4½″. Lightly pencil a line across the length of paper at each set of marks. Following the general instructions for creating tabs (page 12), draft 2 tabs on the bottom of the pop-up and on the bottom ½″ segment, as indicated in the illustration. Draft a tab on the top ½″ row for the box top. Add a crease line to the top flap as shown.

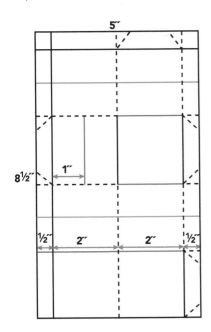

8. Cut out the tabs and score the rest of the drawn lines with a creasing tool.

9. Turn the pop-up paper over and fold it into a 2″ box. Glue the ½″ side tab inside the adjacent edge to form a box with 2 bottom tabs and a top 2″ flap with a ½″ tab.

10. Fold the 2″ flap down and glue the ½″ tab on the flap to the inside of the box.

11. Fold the 2 bottom tabs out. Place the pop-up box onto the front of the backer card. Slide a pop-up tab into each of the cut slits.

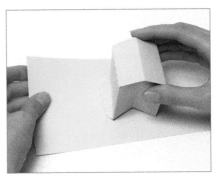

12. Turn the entire piece over and glue the tabs in place. Let the glue dry.

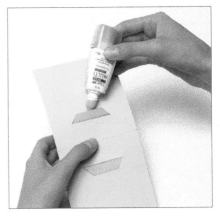

13. Gently fold the pop-up card closed and press it down to ensure straight and tight folds. Reopen the pop-up to see the 180° Cube Pop-Up!

# 180° COIL POP-UP

This pop-up is fun and so easy to create! When the pop-up is finished, both sides of the coil's paper show as it bends from one side to the other.

## Materials

- Basic tools (see pages 7–9)
- 4″ × 8″ piece of backer card
- 4″ × 4″ piece of pop-up paper
- Adhesive

## Assembly

1. On the back of the 4″ × 8″ backer card, measure halfway up from the short bottom edge and pencil a dot on each long edge. Lightly pencil a line from dot to dot across the width of the backer card to create the centerline. Score the centerline with a creasing tool.

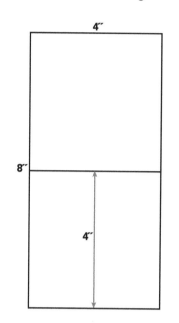

2. Turn the backer card over to the front and fold it in half on the scored line.

3. Lightly trace the coil (template below) onto the 4″ × 4″ pop-up paper.

4. Cut out the coil on the drawn line.

5. Open the backer card. Center the coil on one side of the backer card. Place a small amount of glue on one end of the coil. Press the coil into place and let the glue dry.

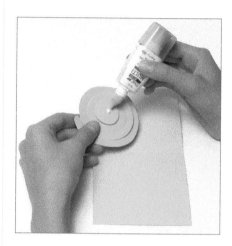

6. Once the glue has dried, open the backer card so the other side of the coil is facing up. Add a drop of glue to the other end of the coil.

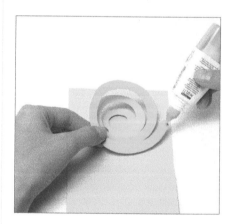

7. Close the backer card over the end of the coil, press, and let the glue dry.

8. Once the glue has dried, open the card and gently spread the coil apart. Fun!

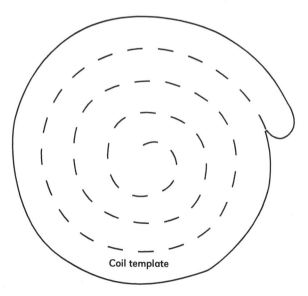

Coil template

# 180° EQUAL ANGLE POP-UP

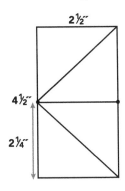

This pop-up is just like the multi-sheet 90° Equal Angle Pop-Up (page 24) except that it works when the card is opened 180° instead of 90°.

## Materials

- Basic tools (see pages 7–9)
- 2½″ × 4½″ piece of pop-up paper
- 4″ × 8″ piece of backer card
- Adhesive

## Assembly

**1.** On the back of the 2½″ × 4½″ pop-up paper, measure halfway up from the short bottom edge and pencil a dot on each long edge. Lightly pencil a line from dot to dot across the width of the paper to create the centerline.

**2.** Lightly pencil a diagonal line from the left edge dot to the upper right corner. Lightly pencil a diagonal line from the left edge dot to the lower right corner.

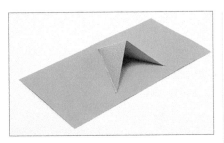

**3.** Following the general instructions for creating tabs (pages 12–13), draft a tab on each angle side.

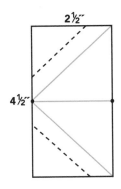

**4.** Score the drawn lines with a creasing tool. Cut out the pop-up piece with a craft knife.

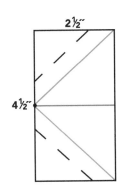

**5.** On the back of the 4″ × 8″ backer card, measure halfway up from the short bottom edge and pencil a dot on each long edge. Lightly pencil a line from dot to dot across the width of the backer card to create the centerline. Score the centerline with a creasing tool.

**6.** Measure ½″ in from each long edge on the centerline and pencil a dot.

**7.** Measure 1½″ above the right centerline dot and pencil a second dot. Measure 1½″ below the right centerline dot and pencil a third dot.

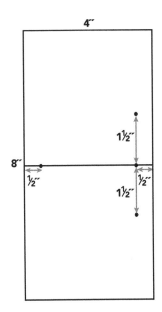

**8.** Lightly pencil a diagonal line from the left centerline dot to the upper right dot. Lightly pencil another diagonal line from the left centerline dot to the lower right dot.

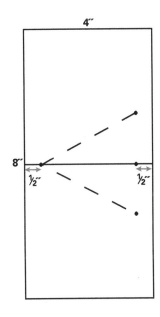

**9.** With a craft knife, cut a slit on each of the 2 angled lines drawn in Step 8.

**10.** Turn the pop-up card over to the front. Insert the pop-up tabs into the cut slits.

**11.** Turn the entire pop-up over to the back and glue the pop-up tabs down to the back of the backer card, pressing them outward. Let the glue dry.

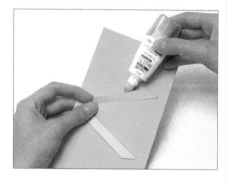

**12.** Close the card and press to ensure straight and tight fold lines. Turn the pop-up over and re open it to see the 180° Equal Angle Pop-Up!

# 180° ARMATURE POP-UP

This pop-up is unique because it works only when another piece is added to it. The 180° Armature Pop-Up is the most basic pop-up armature and is used in many 180° pop-up pieces.

## Materials

- Basic tools (see pages 7–9)
- 2 pieces ¾″ × 3½″ of armature pop-up paper
- 4″ × 8″ piece of backer card
- 4″ × 4″ square of cardstock for the flower
- 2″ × 2″ square of cardstock for the flower center
- Adhesive

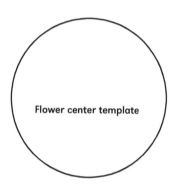

Flower center template

Flower template

## Assembly

**1.** On each ¾″ × 3½″ armature pop-up paper, measure and mark the following points from left to right on each long edge: ½″, 1½″, 2″, and 3″. Lightly pencil a line across the width of the paper at each set of marks. Score the drawn lines with a creasing tool.

|  | 3½″ |  |  |  |  |
|---|---|---|---|---|---|
| ½″ | 1″ | ½″ | 1″ | ½″ | ¾″ |

**2.** Fold each ¾″ × 3½″ strip into a ¾″ × 1″ rectangular armature box. Glue one ½″ tab on top of the other ½″ tab. Set aside.

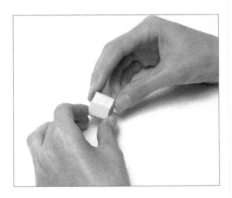

**3.** On the back of the 4″ x 8″ backer card, measure halfway up from the short bottom edge and pencil a dot on each long edge. Lightly pencil a line from dot to dot across the width of the backer card to create the centerline. Measure 1⅝″ in from each long edge on the drawn centerline and pencil a dot. Score the centerline with a creasing tool.

**4.** Except for the dots drawn in Step 3, erase the rest of the drawn lines. Turn the backer card over and fold it on the scored line.

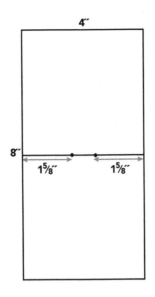

4″

8″

1⅝″    1⅝″

**5.** Glue a ¾″ × 1″ rectangular armature box to the backer card between the drawn dots. The armature edge goes right next to the centerline.

**6.** Repeat Step 5 with the other ¾″ × 1″ armature on the other side of the centerline.

**7.** Trace the flower template onto the 4″ piece of cardstock and the flower center onto the 2″ piece of cardstock. Cut out the shapes with scissors.

**8.** With a creasing tool, score a line through the middle of the flower and through the middle of the flower center. Fold on the scored lines.

**9.** Position the flower center in the middle of the flower with the 2 scored centerlines lining up on top of each other. Glue the flower center to the flower and let the glue dry.

**10.** Apply glue to the top of the armatures on the backer card. Align the flower centerline with the backer card centerline. Press the flower down onto the armatures. Let the glue dry.

**11.** Close the card and press to ensure straight and tight fold lines. Reopen the card to see the finished 180° Armature Pop-Up!

# CHAPTER 6

# Pop-Up Projects

This chapter covers an assortment of projects using the techniques covered in this book. These simple projects are great for practice. Each project focuses on one or two techniques, and I have added embellishments and other decorative products to add zest to the finished pieces.

## Pop-Up Note Cards

Rubber Stamp or Sticker Pop-Up Note Card

Any of the pop-up techniques in this book can be used to create note cards. This project uses a single-sheet 90° Unequal Pop-Up with a 3″ rubber stamp. (Rubber stamps are a great way to add personality or a theme to the pop-ups!) I have included an overview before each step explaining what is being accomplished. This way, you will know how to draft a pop-up using any size stamp!

## Create Any Size 90° Pop-Up Card

### Materials

- Basic tools (see pages 7–9)

- Rubber stamp or sticker that measures about 3″ square

- 4″ × 9″ piece of pop-up paper (for this example)

- 4″ × 9″ piece of backer card (for this example)

- Adhesive

### Backer Card Size

To determine the size of the backer card:

1. Measure the rubber stamp or sticker to be used for the pop-up artwork; then decide how far out the pop-up will extend from the background. Add these measurements together to determine how far up the pop-up will go when the card is closed. For the stamp I chose, the backer card needs to be at least 8″ long, so when it is folded in half it will cover the pop-up.

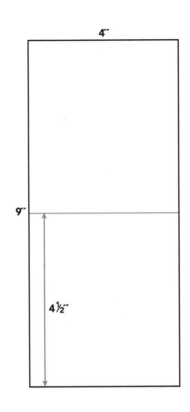

**2.** To calculate the width of the backer card, add at least ½″ to the width of the image. (That is, add at least ¼″ to each side of the image; if the image is 3″ wide, the width of the backer card should be at least 3½″.) For this example, we added a bit to each of the measurements, so we are using a 4″ × 9″ backer card.

**3.** Now that we've determined the backer card size, measure halfway up from the short bottom edge and pencil a dot on each long edge. Lightly pencil a line from dot to dot across the width of the backer card to create the centerline.

## Assembly

**1.** On the back of the 4″ × 9″ pop-up paper, measure halfway up from the short bottom edge and pencil a dot on each long edge. Lightly pencil a line from dot to dot across the width of the paper to create the centerline.

## HOW TO PLACE THE IMAGE

*Decide whether you want the artwork image centered on the card or off center. I leave at least ¼″ of space between the edge of the backer card and the pop-up or between 2 pop-ups on the same card. For this example, the image is centered on the backer card ⅝″ from each edge.*

**2.** Measure ⅝″ in from each long edge on the drawn centerline and pencil a dot.

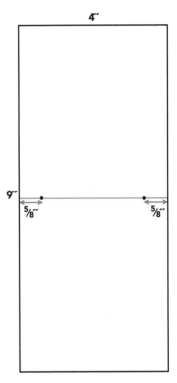

*Decide where you want the artwork image placed on the centerline and mark the width of the image with 2 dots. Measure down from each dot the distance you decided on for the distance between the pop-up and the background and pencil another dot. In this example, the distance is 1″.*

**3.** Measure 1″ down from the left centerline dot and pencil another dot. Repeat with the right centerline dot. Lightly pencil a line between the dots to create the pop-up's bottom line.

**4.** Draw a light line from the bottom line to the dots on the centerline.

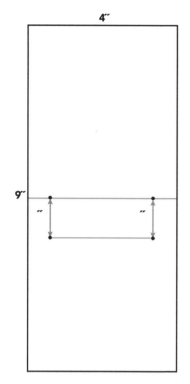

The bottom horizontal line is the bottom lines for the artwork image, and the 2 vertical lines become the sidelines for the image. The image will be placed in this box.

**5.** Align the bottom edge of the rubber stamp or sticker on the bottom drawn line and align the sides of the stamp or sticker with the drawn sidelines. Stamp the image and color as desired, or apply the sticker.

*If the image you are working with does not have a straight line at the top, lightly pencil a line at least ¼″ wide. This line becomes a fold line for the pop-up. Measure up from this line the same distance that you measured down from the centerline for the pop-up's bottom line and pencil a dot on each side. In this example, the distance is 1″. Draw another horizontal line to connect these dots to create the top line of the pop-up.*

**6.** Draw a straight line across the top of the stamped image or the sticker for the pop-up fold line.

**7.** Measure 1″ up from each end of the drawn line and pencil a dot. Draw another line to connect the dots to create the pop-up's top line.

*For the pop-up sidelines, connect the top line of the pop-up with the bottom line of the pop-up. This line does not have to be straight and can follow the contour of the stamp or sticker.*

**8.** Draw vertical lines between the pop-up top lines and bottom lines. With a craft knife, cut on the drawn pop-up sidelines to make the pop-up side slits.

*Now that you've drafted the pop-up card, simply follow the rest of the steps to finish the example. You can put as many pop-ups on the same card as the backer card width will allow!*

**9.** Draw the backer card centerline to meet up to the pop-up sidelines. Score the drawn horizontal lines with a creasing tool. Erase all the pencil lines.

**10.** Gently pull the center cut area toward you. Crease a mountain fold on the pop-up centerline and valley folds on the background centerline and the top and bottom horizontal pop-up lines.

**11.** Fold the pop-up completely closed and press it down on a flat surface to ensure straight and tight folds. Reopen the pop-up to see the finished Rubber Stamp or Sticker Pop-Up Note Card.

# Bouquet of Flowers Pop-Up

This note card combines several pop-up techniques to make one piece. The 180° Armature Pop-Up is used here, along with the 180° Angled Pop-Up (often used as a mouth). This is a great project to alter to fit your tastes. For starters, instead of a bouquet of flowers, you could create an ice cream cone!

## Materials

- Basic tools (see pages 7–9)
- 2 pieces 4½″ × 8″ of backer card
- 2½″ × 4″ piece of vase pop-up paper
- 2 pieces ⅜″ × 2½″ of armature pop-up paper
- 3 pieces 3″ × 3″ of flower paper; 1 each in pink, yellow, and orange
- 6 stems (cut ³⁄₁₆″ × 1½″ stems from green paper)
- Adhesive
- 1½″ square flower rubber stamp
- Purple embossing powder
- Embossing inkpad
- Heat tool
- 2″ edge punch

## Assembly

**1.** On the back of one of the 4½″ × 8″ backer cards, measure halfway up from the short bottom edge and pencil a dot on each long edge. Lightly pencil a line from dot to dot across the width of the backer card to create the centerline. Score the centerline with a creasing tool. Turn the backer card over to the front and fold it in half on the scored line.

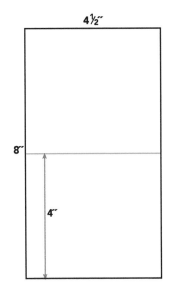

**2.** Open the backer card. On the back, measure ½″ in from the left edge and pencil a first light dot on the centerline. Measure 3¼″ in from the left edge and pencil a second dot. Measure and pencil a third dot 1½″ above the second dot and a fourth dot 1½″ below the second dot (creating a 60° angle).

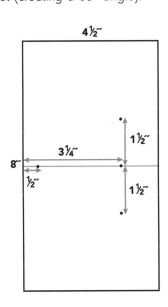

**3.** Lightly pencil a diagonal line from the first dot to the third dot. Lightly pencil a diagonal line from the first dot to the fourth dot. With a craft knife, cut the 2 angle lines to create a **V** slot. Set aside.

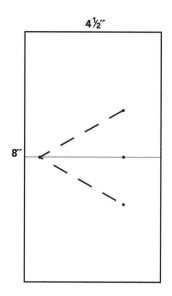

**4.** On pop-up paper, measure halfway up from the short bottom edge and pencil a dot on each long edge. Lightly pencil a line from dot to dot across the width of the paper to create the centerline.

**5.** Lightly pencil a diagonal line from the left edge dot to the **upper** right corner. Lightly pencil another diagonal line from the left edge dot to the **lower** right corner.

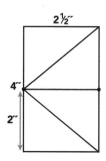

**6.** Following the general instructions for creating tabs (pages 12–13),

draft a tab on each angle side on the vase pop-up paper.

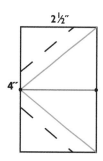

**7.** Cut out the vase pop-up piece along the tabs. Score the drawn lines with a creasing tool.

**8.** With the edge punch, punch the design along the long edge of the pop-up piece. Set aside.

**9.** With both ⅜″ × 2½″ armature pieces, follow the instructions for creating 180° Armature Pop-Ups (page 42). Measure both pieces into 5 increments, ½″ each. Score and glue each armature together. Set aside.

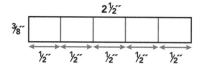

**10.** Stamp 4 flowers each on the 3 colored flower papers (12 flowers total) with the flower rubber stamp and embossing inkpad. Follow the embossing powder manufacturer's instructions to finish each flower with purple embossing powder and a heat tool. Cut out all the flowers.

**11.** Referring to the project photo (page 47), glue 3 flowers together for the pop-up. Measure across the center of the combined flowers and score a vertical line on the middle flower. Gently fold the combined flowers in half.

**12.** Open up the flowers and glue a stem to the bottom of the individual flowers. Be sure the center stem is positioned off to one side and does not hit the vertical scored line.

**13.** Glue the 2 armature pieces from Step 9 to the back of the flowers, one on each edge of the centerline. Let the glue dry.

**14.** Following the instructions for the 180° Equal Angle Pop-Up (page 41), position and glue the vase piece from Step 8 in place.

**15.** Position the flowers in the vase with the armatures ½″ down from the top edge of the card. Following the instructions for the 180° Armature Pop-Ups (page 42), glue the armatures in place onto the backer card.

**16.** On the back of the second 4½″ × 8″ backer card, measure halfway up from the short bottom edge and pencil a dot on each long edge. Lightly pencil a line from dot to dot across the width of the backer card to create the centerline. Score the centerline with a creasing tool. This will become the outer cover for the pop-up card.

**17.** Fold the outer cover closed on the scored line. Position the pop-up card with the flowers into this outer cover to ensure that it fits. Make any necessary adjustments; then glue the 2 together.

**18.** Glue the extra flowers to the inside and front of the card as desired.

# Pop-Up House

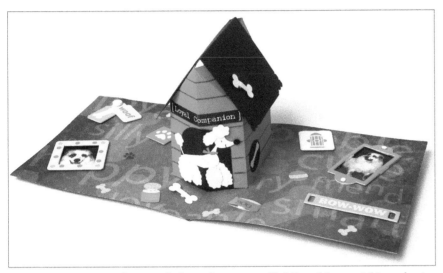

Here is great project . . . decorate the house however you like! One of the great things about pop-ups is that they can be created using themed paper and embellished with any accents you wish. I've created a haunted house, a gingerbread house, and a doghouse . . . but what about a Victorian house for a wedding card or a clubhouse for a child's birthday?

## Materials

- Basic tools (see pages 7–9)
- 2 pieces 6″ × 12″ of backer card paper
- 4½″ × 10½″ house pop-up paper
- 3¼″ × 5¼″ large roof piece
- 3″ × 5″ medium roof piece
- Decorative corner punch
- Adhesive

## Assembly

1. On the back of a 6″ × 12″ backer card, measure halfway up from the short bottom edge and pencil a dot on each long edge.

Lightly pencil a line from dot to dot across the width of the paper to create the centerline. Score the centerline with a creasing tool. Turn the card over and fold it in half on the scored line.

2. Measure 1¾″ in from each long edge on the drawn centerline and pencil a dot.

3. Measure 1¼″ up from the **left** centerline dot and pencil a third dot. Measure 1¼″ up from the **right** centerline dot and pencil a fourth dot.

4. Lightly pencil a line between the 1¼″ dots above the centerline to create the top line.

5. Repeat Steps 3 and 4, now measuring **below** the centerline.

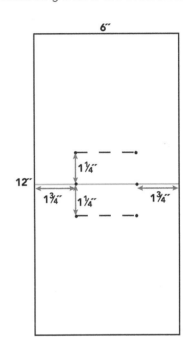

6. With a craft knife, cut on both the top line and the bottom line to make the pop-up slots. Set aside.

7. On the 4½″ × 10½″ house pop-up paper, measure and mark the following points on each long edge, from left to right: ½″, 3″, 4¼″, 5½″, 8″, and 9¼″. Lightly pencil a line across the width of the paper at each set of marks.

8. Measure and mark the following points on each short edge of the house pop-up paper: ½″, 3″, and 4¼″. Lightly pencil a line across the length of the paper at each set of marks.

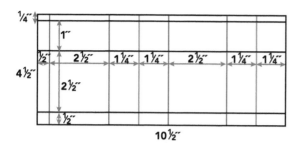

**9.** Referring to the illustration, draft the roof slopes and the tabs for the roof slopes, the sides, and the bottom of the house.

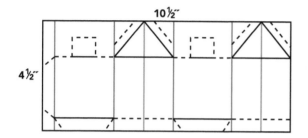

**10.** Cut out the house pop-up and score the fold lines.

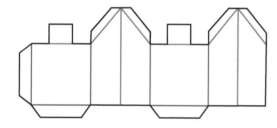

**11.** With the decorative corner punch, punch each corner of the large and medium roof pieces. Measure halfway up from the short bottom edge of each roof piece and pencil a dot on each long edge for the centerlines. Score the centerline of each roof piece with a creasing tool.

**12.** Center the medium roof piece on top of the large roof piece and glue in place.

**13.** Embellish and decorate the house and roof as desired. Be sure not to add an embellishment that cannot be folded on any fold lines.

**14.** Glue the side tab on the house pop-up to the inside of the adjacent edge to form the house.

**15.** Glue the roof to the house by gluing the glue tabs drafted in Step 10 to the back of the roof.

**16.** Insert the bottom tabs on the house pop-up into the slots cut on the backer card.

**17.** Gently close the backer card with the pop-up house and glue the house tab to the backer card. Turn the card over and glue the other tab to the backer card. Let the glue dry.

**18.** On the back of the second 6″ × 12″ backer card, measure halfway up from the short bottom edge and pencil a dot on each long edge. Lightly pencil a line from dot to dot across the width of the backer card to create the centerline. Score the centerline with a creasing tool. This will become the outer cover for the pop-up card.

**19.** Fold the outer cover closed on the scored line. Position the pop-up card into this outer cover to ensure that it fits. Make any necessary adjustments; then glue the 2 together.

**20.** Open the backer card and embellish the card as desired.

**Vary the design for holidays!**

# Pop-Up Gift Tags

## PRESENT

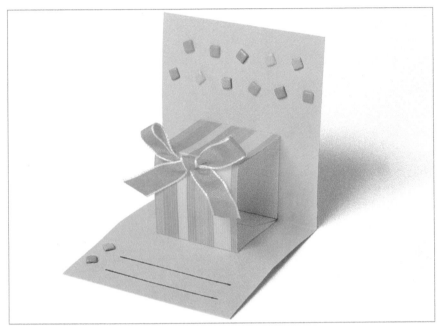

These little gift tags are simple to make and can easily be customized for a variety of holidays just by changing the colors or prints of the paper you use. How delightful it would be to give an extra pop-up surprise with your next gift!

### Materials

- Basic tools (see pages 7-9)
- 1½" × 6½" piece of pop-up paper
- 2 pieces 3" × 6½" of backer card paper
- 8" of ¼" ribbon
- Assorted ⅜" square colored fasteners
- Adhesive

### Assembly

**1.** On the back of the 1½" × 6½" pop-up paper, measure and mark the following points on each long edge, from left to right: 1½", 3", 4½", and 6". Lightly pencil a line across the width of the paper at each set of marks.

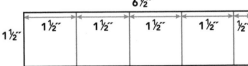

**2.** On the back of the 3" × 6½" backer card, measure halfway up from the short bottom edge and pencil a dot on each long edge. Lightly pencil a line from dot to dot across the width of the backer card to create the centerline. Score the centerline with a creasing tool. Turn the card over and fold on the scored line.

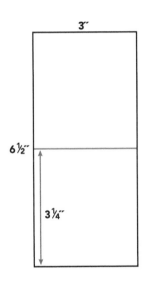

**3.** Follow the instructions for the multi-sheet 90° Equal Parallel Pop-Up (page 17) to assemble the pop-up.

**4.** Tie the ribbon into a bow. Glue the bow to the front of the pop-up box. Let the glue dry.

**5.** Decide how you would like to place the paper fasteners across the top of the gift tag. Lightly mark each spot with a pencil dot. (It's best to leave at least ¼" between the dots.)

6. Punch a small hole through each of the dots with an awl.

7. Push the fasteners into the holes.

8. On the bottom edge of the backer card, draw 2 lines ½″ apart, ½″ in from each edge of the backer card, and ½″ up from the bottom of the backer card.

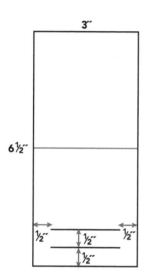

9. Punch a hole at the beginning of each line with an awl. Add a square fastener to each hole.

10. On the back of the second 3″ x 6½″ backer card, measure halfway up from the short bottom edge and pencil a dot on each long edge. Lightly pencil a line from dot to dot across the width of the backer card to create the centerline. Score the centerline with a creasing tool. This will become the outer cover for the pop-up card.

11. Fold the outer cover closed on the scored line. Position the pop-up card into this outer cover to ensure that it fits. Make any necessary adjustments; then glue the 2 together.

# CHRISTMAS TREE

## Materials

- Basic tools (see pages 7–9)
- ½″ x 4½″ piece of pop-up paper
- 2 pieces 3″ x 6½″ of backer card
- 3″ x 3″ piece of green paper
- 1″ x 1″ piece of yellow paper
- ½″ x 1″ piece of brown paper (for the trunk)
- Adhesive
- Assorted ⅛″ round colored fasteners
- ³⁄₁₆″ glue dots
- Silver microfine glitter—ProvoCraft
- ½″ Christmas tree punch
- ½″ star punch

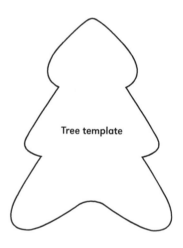

Tree template

## Assembly

1. On the back of the ½″ x 4½″ pop-up paper, measure and mark the following points on each long edge, from left to right: 1″, 2″, 3″, and 4″. Lightly pencil a line across the width of the paper at each set of marks.

2. Score the drawn lines with a creasing tool.

| 1″ | 1″ | 1″ | 1″ | ½″ |
|---|---|---|---|---|

3. Turn the pop-up paper over to the front and mountain fold each crease line to create a box. Apply glue to the ½″ tab and glue it to the inside of the adjacent edge to form a ½″ × 1″ box.

4. On the back of the 3″ × 6½″ backer card, measure halfway up from the short bottom edge and pencil a dot on each long edge. Lightly pencil a line from dot to dot across the width of the backer card to create the centerline. Score the centerline with a creasing tool. Turn the card over and fold on the scored line.

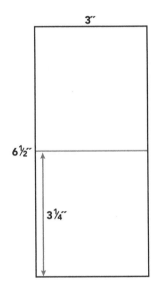

5. Trace the tree template onto the green paper and cut it out.

6. Punch out a ½″ star from the yellow paper with the star paper punch.

7. Glue the star to the top of the tree. Be sure the star does not stick up more than ⅛″ above the top of the tree.

8. Center the brown paper trunk on the back of the tree. The trunk should stick out ⅜″ to ½″ below the tree. Glue the trunk to the tree.

9. Pencil some dots on the tree for the fasteners. Punch a hole on each dot with an awl.

10. Push the fasteners into the holes for the ornaments.

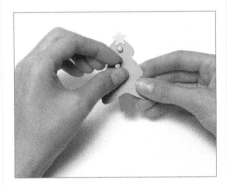

11. Align the tree on the front of the pop-up piece, making sure the bottom of the trunk is flush with the bottom of the pop-up edge. Glue the tree to the pop-up piece.

12. Center the tree pop-up on the backer card and glue in place, following the instructions for the multi-sheet 90° Equal Parallel Pop-Up (page 17). Let the glue dry.

13. Randomly place the glue dots around the tree on the front of the backer card.

14. Sprinkle glitter over the glue dots to cover them completely. Shake off any excess glitter.

15. On the bottom edge of the backer card starting 1″ from the bottom, pen in 2 horizontal lines ½″ apart, starting ¾″ in from the left edge and ending ½″ in from the right edge.

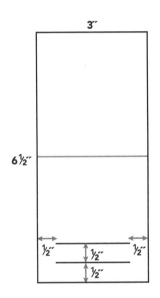

16. Punch 2 trees from the green paper using the Christmas tree punch. Glue a tree at the left edge of the 2 horizontal lines you drew in Step 15.

# CANDLES

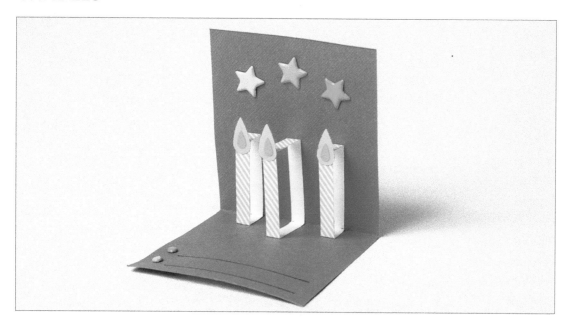

## Materials

- Basic tools (see pages 7–9)
- ¼" × 5½" piece of pop-up paper
- 2 pieces ¼" × 4½" of pop-up paper
- 2 pieces 3" × 6½" of backer card paper
- 2" × 2" square of yellow paper
- 1" × 1" square of pink paper
- Adhesive
- ½" teardrop punch
- ¼" teardrop punch
- 3 assorted ½" colored star fasteners
- 2 assorted ⅛" colored round fasteners

## Assembly

**1.** On the back of the ¼" × 5½" pop-up paper, measure and mark the following points on each long edge, from left to right: 1", 2½", 3½", and 5". Lightly pencil a line across the width of the paper at each set of marks. Score the drawn lines with a creasing tool.

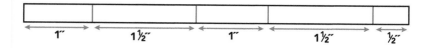

**2.** Turn the ¼" × 5½" pop-up paper over to the front and mountain fold each crease line to create a 1" box. Apply glue to the ½" tab and glue the tab to the inside of the adjacent 1" edge to form a ¼" × 1½" candle.

**3.** On the back of both pieces of ¼" × 4½" pop-up paper, measure and mark the following points on each long edge, from left to right: ½", 2", 2½", and 4". Lightly pencil a line across the width of the papers at each set of marks.

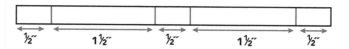

**4.** Score the drawn lines with a creasing tool.

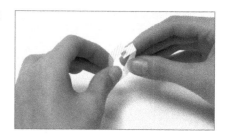

**5.** Turn the ¼˝ × 4½˝ pop-up papers over to the front and mountain fold each scored line to create two 1˝ boxes. Apply glue to the ½˝ tabs and glue the tabs to the insides of the adjacent ½˝ edges to form two ½˝ × 1½˝ candles. You now have a total of 3 candles.

**6.** On the back of the 3˝ × 6½˝ backer card, measure halfway up from the short bottom edge and pencil a dot on each long edge. Lightly pencil a line from dot to dot across the width of the backer card to create the centerline. Score the centerline with a creasing tool.

**7.** Center the 3 candle pop-ups onto the backer card and, referring to the photo, glue them in place.

**8.** Punch three ½˝ teardrops from the yellow paper.

**9.** Punch three ¼˝ teardrops from the pink paper.

**10.** Glue a ¼˝ pink teardrop onto the center of a ½˝ yellow teardrop to create a candle flame. Repeat to make 3 candle flames.

**11.** Glue a flame to the top of each candle pop-up.

**12.** Pencil 3 dots above the candles for the star fasteners. Punch a hole on each of the pencil marks with an awl. Push a star fastener into each hole.

**13.** On the bottom edge of the backer card starting 1˝ from the bottom, pen in 2 horizontal lines, ½˝ apart, starting ¾˝ in from the left edge and ending ½˝ in from the right edge.

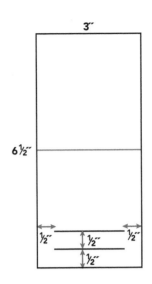

**14.** Punch a hole at the beginning of each line with an awl. Add a ⅛˝ round fastener to each hole.

**15.** On the back of the second 3˝ x 6½˝ backer card, measure halfway up from the short bottom edge and pencil a dot on each long edge. Lightly pencil a line from dot to dot across the width of the backer card to create the centerline. Score the centerline with a creasing tool. This will become the outer cover for the pop-up card.

**16.** Fold the outer cover closed on the scored line. Position the pop-up card into this outer cover to ensure that it fits. Make any necessary adjustments; then glue the 2 together.

# Pop-Up Books

We have covered a variety of techniques and embellishments, and they can all be combined to create a pop-up book! There are many kinds of pop-up books, but the one thing they have in common is that each book has its own theme. To create a pop-up book, first you have to pick that theme. In this section, I've included examples of charm books, memory books, and children's books, all with construction tips.

## TYPES OF POP-UP BOOKS

Any book that would be illustrated can be a pop-up book. I have included examples of three types of pop-up books to start with.

### Charm Book

This tiny charm book can be given to someone as a little piece of inspiration. Give a charm book in place of a greeting card. Select a small blank book that will fit in an envelope and mail it to someone to brighten his or her day. Create charm books to use as favors at a wedding or baby shower.

### Memory Book

**Memory Book by Sharon Cheng**

A memory book is a stand-alone scrapbook. Create one to remember a special event or to give as a thank you gift for someone deserving. Memory books are fun to make and can be designed just like scrapbook pages. There are many books and magazines that share tips on the best way to lay out pages with photographs. Check some of these out when designing your memory book.

Children's pop-up books are designed to entertain and, sometimes, to educate the reader. To create a children's pop-up book, think of a theme that will entertain the recipient. Perhaps write a short story and then create pop-ups to illustrate the book. Create an alphabet book and use pop-up pictures that start with certain letters. A counting theme is a great one to use when making a pop-up book.

## Children's Book

### Artwork

Once you have picked the type of book and theme for your pop-up book, you will need to find or create the artwork for the book. Look for designs printed on scrapbook paper, coloring books, or greeting or note cards. For the memory books, look for photos to use and embellishments to accent them. As you saw in the section on note cards, rubber stamps and stickers are also excellent sources. If you like to design your own artwork, you can scan it into a computer, scale it to the appropriate size, and print it on photo paper or cardstock.

## Book Structure

A pop-up book needs a blank book to be built on. You have two choices: buy a blank book or create your own book. I recommend buying one that has already been cut and bound. **Ready-To-Go! Blank Board Books** by Create & Treasure (see Sources, page 64) are wonderful to work with and come in assorted sizes and colors. If you choose to make your own blank book, you will need to buy heavy-duty chipboard. Lightweight chipboard will warp when glue is applied to it, and it may bend from the weight of the pop-ups. There are great how-to books on making your own blank book. I recommend reading some of these before making your own blank book.

## Embellishments

When selecting embellishments for a pop-up book, keep in mind the thickness of the embellishment. Just as for pop-up cards, you want to pick embellishments that will allow the pop-up piece to close. Thickness is especially important when making a pop-up book because you are stacking the various pop-up pages on top of one another. Also if you are using a lot of embellishments, they will cause the pop-up book to remain partly open. If this happens to a project you are working on, consider

a tie or band that will fit around the book as part of the design.

**Band closure**

## Selecting Pop-Up Structures

When designing your pop-up book, look at the different pop-up techniques. You can use an assortment of 90° and 180° pop-ups in the same book. Select a combination of techniques that vary in thickness. As for the embellishments, the thickness of the pop-ups has to be considered. A pop-up with a lot of pieces is already pretty thick, so try to keep the embellishments flat. You can add more embellishments to a simple pop-up.

# CREATING A POP-UP BOOK

## Cover It With Paper

In all the examples shown in this book, the blank pages of the board books have been covered with assorted papers. Covering the pages sounds like a simple step, but there are some pitfalls to avoid.

Unlike pop-up cards, which have only one crease along the centerline, books have two small crease lines about 1/16" apart. This space between these two lines is called the gutter. If you cover a page spread and the gutter with one piece of paper the book will not open to 180° once the glue on the paper has dried. There are different ways to work around this problem. For beginners, I recommend applying one sheet of paper to each half of the page spread. Butt each sheet of paper up to the gutter but not over it. This method will give you a 1/16" gap where the blank book will show through. You can color in this space, choose a blank book in a color that goes with the project you are working on, or leave the gap showing.

**Page covered with a sheet**

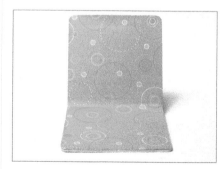

**Page spread covered with a sheet**

## Gluing the Paper

I always complete the inside pages of a pop-up book first before covering the cover. As you work on a book, you will handle it quite a bit, and you can easily get glue, ink, or other materials on the cover. There is nothing worse than finishing the inside of the book only to close it and see that there is something all over the cover. If you complete the cover last, it will not matter if some other material manages to jump onto the cover uninvited.

1. To size paper to cover a page inside a blank book, trace the page on the back of the paper you are going to use. For an inside page, add at least ½″ on 3 sides. For the cover, add ½″ on all 4 sides. Adding the extra ½″ on the sides will make trimming the paper to the edge of the book page much easier.

2. When gluing the paper to the book, apply the adhesive to the blank book page rather than to the paper. The blank book is made from a heavy cardboard and is less likely to warp when exposed to a layer of glue. The paper, which is thinner, will most definitely warp and wrinkle when you apply glue to it. Add a very thin layer of glue to cover the majority of the book page, including all the edges. The more glue you add, the more likely the paper is to warp once it is added to the blank page.

3. Center the paper on the blank page, butting the paper up to the gutter crease in the center of the book. Smooth the paper down into place and close the book onto the paper to help press it down.

4. Using a craft knife with a new blade, carefully trim the paper flush with the edges of the book. Use the edges of the book like a ruler to keep the cuts straight. A sharp blade is very important for this step. A dull blade will drag along the edge of the paper and tear it instead of cutting it, making a mess of the paper you just carefully added to your book.

Trimming the paper to the edge of the book

## Creating a Cover

Once the inside pages are finished, you are ready to add paper to the cover. Here it is okay to use a single piece of paper to cover the front, spine, and back of the book.

1. Place the open book on the back of the cover paper and trace around the edges.

Tracing the book cover

2. Cut the paper ½″ larger on all 4 sides than the dimensions necessary to cover the front and back covers and the spine of the book.

Add ½″ to the cover sheet.

3. Start on one edge and glue the paper to the front cover. Trim the paper for only that side before moving on to the spine of the book.

4. Glue the paper to the spine of the book and then glue the paper to the back cover.

## Tabs in Pop-Up Books

When you construct a pop-up book, you'll deal with tabs differently than for a pop-up card. In a pop-up card, the backer card usually has a slot cut in it for the tabs on the pop-up to fit into, and the tabs are glued to the back of the backer card. When you construct a pop-up book, you stick the tabs under the pop-up and glue them to the top of the blank book page. This method is used because unlike a pop-up card, a page in a book is shared with the pop-up you are working on and the pop-up that will go on the next page.

# Ideas & Inspiration

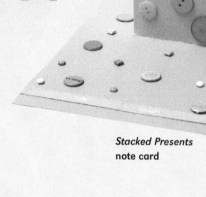

**Stacked Presents**
note card

**Beach Party**
scrapbook page
by Stacey Ann Lorish

**Doggy Days**
scrapbook page
by Stacey Ann Lorish

**Sweet Darling**
scrapbook page
by Stacey Ann Lorish

*Fun in the Sun* charm book

*Pure Bliss* charm book

# CONCLUSION

Throughout this book, you have seen how fun and easy it is to create pop-up art. There are many other great techniques for creating pop-ups that I could not fit in this book. Paper engineering, like other types of engineering, has so much potential to be able to build on what has already been discovered to create a new and unique pop-up piece. So whether you are aiming to be the next great paper engineer or you just want to add some pop to your projects, I hope this book has inspired you!

# ABOUT THE AUTHOR

**Heidi Pridemore** was born and raised in Rochester, New York. She is a graduate of Rochester Institute of Technology (RIT), where she earned a Bachelor of Fine Arts degree in Industrial Design. Upon graduating from RIT, Heidi went to work in the craft industry, where she designed over 200 products for the educational market, using a variety of media. During this time, Heidi gained invaluable experience writing and illustrating instructions for people of varying skills and age levels.

In 1998 Heidi moved to Arizona, where she started her own business designing pop-up art for commercial use. Over time, her business moved on to specialize in designing projects for the quilting and fabric industry. Though she has gone on to become a well-known quilt and fabric designer, she has never forgotten her passion for designing dimensional art from paper and how enjoyable it is to design die-cut pieces that fold up into whatever shape she desires. She is thrilled to return to her roots and share her knowledge of papercrafts.

Best known for her whimsical and unique quilts and fabrics in dramatic, bright colors, Heidi has created quilts for a number of fabric companies, including Blank Quilting, Robert Kaufman, Michael Miller, and Clothworks. Her work has been published in a variety of magazines, such as *Quiltmaker*, *McCall's Quilting*, and *Quilter's World Magazine*. She has also designed fabric lines for Fabri-Quilt and Blank Quilting.

Heidi spends much of her time designing, traveling to trade shows and lectures, and running workshops, but when she's not traveling, she lives in Arizona with her husband, Matthew, and their dog, Cleo.

# SOURCES

**AmericanPin/HyGlo**

*Assorted fasteners, scissors, punches, and other office supplies*

P.O. Box 7340

Tempe, AZ 85281

800-821-7125

www.americanpin.com

www.hyglocrafts.com

**ProvoCraft**

*Embellishments and products perfect for pop-ups*

151 East 3450 North

Spanish Fork, UT 84660

800-937-7686

www.provocraft.com

**Ready-to-Go Blank Board Books!**

*Blank board books in a multitude of acid-free sizes, shapes, and colors*

Create & Treasure

1651 Challenge Dr.

Concord, CA 94520

800-284-1114

www.blankboardbooks.com

**The Whimsical Workshop LLC**

*A variety of fabrics, kits, and patterns for both beginner and advanced quilters*

1050 E. Ray Rd. #A5-166

Chandler, AZ 85225

888-499-5715

www.thewhimsicalworkshop.com